If you don't
make a name
for yourself,
someone
will make
one for you.

If you don't
make a name
for yourself,
someone
will make
one for you.

Make a name for yourself.

55 Strategies to Fast-Track Your Professional Prowess

By Scott Ginsberg
(that guy with the nametag)

Make a name for yourself.

Scott Ginsberg
Copyright © 2007 HELLO, my name is Scott!

Printed in the United States of America.

Cover design by
Sue Sylvia of Staircase Press Design

Text layout by
Jeff Braun of TriFecta Creative
www.trifectacreative.com

Edited by
Jessica "That Bagel Girl" Adams

ISBN: 0-9726497-3-5

Table of Contents

29. Focus on the umbrella.

30. Networking works.

31. Word of mouth works.

32. Everything is a plus.

33. Disarm immediate preoccupation.

34. Love the haters.

35. Grow thicker skin.

36. Lessons learned from a job that sucked.

37. Stand out, but don't sell out.

38. Remove what robs you.

39. Happiness is _____.

40. Boxes are for suckers.

41. Write everything down.

42. Make your own music.

43. That's how I roll.

44. Authenticity, not charisma.

45. On being on.

46. On being a sleeper.

47. On just being.

48. Somebody is always watching.

49. But deep down, he's a really nice guy.

50. Friendly always wins.

51. Wait for nothing.

52. You always have a choice.

53. Three words of advice.

54. Food for thought.

55. It's not about the nametag.

A quick story about the greatest day of my life.

Tuesday, April 29th, 2003.

5:47 AM.

The corner of 6th and Morrison.

The air was wet and cold. I was the only person around for three blocks, anxiously awaiting the 5:50 train to take me to the Portland airport.

To my amazement, I was off to New York City for the biggest interview of my career. In less than 24 hours, I would appear on the *CBS Early Show* before an audience of five million people to talk about my new book, *HELLO, my name is Scott.*

Suffice it to say, I was FREAKING out.

In my left hand: an overnight suitcase full of books.
In my right hand: a copy of *USA Today*.

Here's what the major headlines were on that day:
  • Identity theft cases rise this month
  • 75 million Americans living without health insurance
  • Luther Vandross catches pneumonia after stroke
  • SARS outbreak troubles China workers
  • The end of Buffy feels like a dagger to the heart
  • War letters from the Iraqi front lines
  • Cost of AIDS drugs increasing for poor nations
  • Studies find disturbing amounts of contamination in lettuce
  • Hubble telescope catches approaching storm of turbulent gases
  • Man wears nametag for a friendlier society

OK, now, what's wrong with this picture?

Or maybe I should ask, "What's *right* with this picture?"

Because at that exact moment, my twenty-three year-old mind realized something:

Oh. My. God. This is it.
This is what I'm supposed
to do with my life.

This is how I will make a name for myself.

A quick story about why I wrote this book.

HELLO, my name is Scott!

I'm that guy who wears a nametag 24-7 to make people friendlier.

Honestly, it all started out as an experiment seven years ago. One morning when I was a junior at Miami University in Ohio, I had an idea: **what if I left my nametag on all day?**

I wondered how people might react.

Sure enough, I left that nametag on for the entire day.

And people were friendlier.
The silence was broken.
Approachability was in the air!

Complete strangers would yell from across the hall, "What's up Scott?"

I must have met twenty new people in that first day.

Later on that night I returned to my apartment. I stood in front of my bathroom mirror and took a long, hard look at that nametag.

And **two thoughts** occurred to me:

NUMBER 1: Wow! Look how easy it was to encourage approachability among new people!

NUMBER 2: Hmm. You know, if wearing a nametag worked for ONE day, I bet it would work EVERY day.

And so, it came to pass on November 2nd of 2000, that I made THE crucial decision of my entire career:

I vowed to wear a nametag all day, every day, for the rest of my life.

And the rest, as they say, is history.

Which brings us to today.

I now run a successful company, appropriately called *HELLO, my name is Scott*.

My job as an entrepreneur is to help businesspeople make a name for themselves – one conversation at a time. I do so through books, speaking engagements, syndicated columns, newsletters, blogs and online learning tools.

However, I think it's important to tell you:

I am not a doctor.
I am not a coach.
I am not a consultant.
I am not a self-help guru.
I am not a motivational speaker.

I never lost an arm.
I never climbed Everest.
I never overcame tremendous obstacles.

I don't have 20 years of corporate experience.
I don't have a Masters degree.
I don't have a PhD.

(In fact, I don't have a single acronym after my last name!)

Look. I'm just ... a guy. A guy who wears a nametag everyday to make people friendlier.

That's about it.

You see, ever since I transformed my simple idea into a career, I've noticed a trend. Friends, clients and even the media have been telling me (jokingly, I think), "Boy Scott, you've really made a name for yourself!"

Very funny.

But, I suppose it's true; both literally and metaphorically.

So the reason I wrote this book is simple:

I want to help you to
make a name for yourself too.

Whether you're a seasoned professional starting a new job, a recent college graduate searching for a career, or a solo entrepreneur like me, I want to help. Because I truly believe that what I've learned – not what I've done – will be a valuable asset to your professional success.

In the next 220 pages, you're going to learn A BUNCH OF REALLY GOOD IDEAS that will fast track your professional prowess.

No "Seven Steps."
No "Proven Systems."
No formulas.

Just things I've learned from stuff I've done.

From attitude to setting goals to embracing criticism, these ideas are tried and true. I've lived and worked by them for years.

PLEASE NOTE: You don't have to read this book straight through. Feel free to bounce around.

ALSO NOTE: If you're not holding a pen right now, go get one. Inspiration comes unannounced.

FINAL NOTE: If you're reading this book at your desk, I suggest you link up to www.hellomynameisscott.com and other sites on The Nametag Network. There, you will find thousands of resources to supplement your reading that will further enhance your ability to make a name for yourself.

Are you ready?

Cool. Let's do this.

Scott Ginsberg
November 2006
St. Louis, Missouri

A quick story about the dedication.

On September 9, 2006, I gave a talk to 1,800 salespeople in Salt Lake City. After the program was over, a woman I'd never met before approached me with tears in her eyes. She gave me a hug and the single greatest compliment I've ever received:

"Scott, I want to meet your parents!"

Mom, Dad, this book is for you.

You better lose yourself
in the music, the moment.

You own it.
You better never let it go.

You only get one shot.
Do not miss your chance to blow.

This opportunity comes
once in a lifetime.

— *Slim Shady* —

Create a reputation
that accurately
describes you,
often precedes
you and humbly
serves you.

Make a name
for yourself.

*"If you don't make a name for yourself,
someone will make one for you."*

Scott Ginsberg

The first thing you need to do is discover the answer — your answer — to this question:

Why do you want to make a name for yourself?

Possible answers might include (but aren't limited to):
- To become famous or recognized by important people
- To become well known and respected for doing something in particular
- To use the abilities and gifts you've been given
- To validate your existence
- To carve out your name in the minds of everyone you meet
- To be remembered for something
- To leave a legacy
- To develop a signature style
- To discover your voice
- To work without having to sell so much
- To awake each morning vitalized, prepared and ready
- To do something great
- To earn the respect and recognition you deserve
- To blow your boss away
- To be your own boss
- To maximize your experience within a certain time
- To achieve status as an accomplished, credible professional
- To create a reputation that accurately describes you, often precedes you and humbly serves you when you're not there

Now it's your turn:

I WANT TO MAKE A NAME FOR MYSELF SO THAT I CAN…

_____

_____

_____

Name: _____   Date: _____

Cool. With that in mind, let's figure out how to get there …

People buy people first.

"Each and every time you go for it,
make sure you take yourself —
because that's who they asked to see."

Bill Cosby

I'd just finished a speech with a group of sales managers. After everyone cleared out of the room, my client came up to me with a huge smile on his face.

"Great job Scott! I've been getting awesome feedback from my staff. You truly resonated with the team."

"Cool, that's what I like to hear," I replied.

Steve sat down in the chair in front of me. He leaned back, put his feet up and said, "You know Scott, I gotta be honest. I hire a lot of outside trainers just like yourself. And as valuable as your message of approachability was, the *real reason* I chose you...

...is because I liked you **first as a person**; and **second as a professional**."

Wow. Just like that. *Because he liked me.*

LESSON LEARNED: **People buy people first**.

Before your company.
Before your products.
Before your services.

They buy YOU first.

Before your ideas.
Before your suggestions.
Before your work.

They buy YOU first.

THEREFORE: You owe it to yourself to put your values before vocation. Beliefs before business. Person before profession. Individuality before industry.

Here's how. I call it...

The ABC's of Leading with Your Person:

A is for attitude.

Sun Tzu said, "What you believe about yourself, the world will believe about you."

So, before you sell a product, idea or service, first sell yourself on yourself. Because if you don't like you first, nobody else will.

> ## LET ME ASK YA THIS...
>
> How much time do you spend each day selling yourself to yourself? (I suggest one hour each day. We'll talk about this more later.)

B is for breathing.

Breathing your person through every possible touch point, that is. The way you answer the phone, type emails, engage in person, or appear on paper – all of these are different channels through which you have an opportunity to communicate your person FIRST.

C is for consistency.

Ever run into one of your coworkers outside of the office and think, "Oh my God! Jackie from Accounting? She's like a completely different person!"

> ## LET ME ASK YA THIS...
>
> Do your communication channels define you by what you do or who you are?

It's a bummer when that happens. I see it a lot. Not exactly consistent, huh?

Now I know, some people work in jobs that require them to be someone different compared to who they are when they're off the clock.

Yeah. Those people should find new jobs.

Attitude.

Breathing.

Consistency.

That's how you lead with your person. Got it?

Awesome.

Now, speaking of selling yourself to yourself...

LET ME ASK YA THIS...
When was the last time someone
told you "tone down" your real self?

Because you said so.

"*Since you must sell yourself before selling your goods, you must sell yourself on yourself. So believe in yourself.*"

Norman Vincent Peale

The central principle upon which the entire self-help industry is based is: "As a man thinketh, so is he."

I know. Totally cliché, right? Typical self-help answer. Start with attitude.

But it's true.

You can't make a name for yourself unless you have an awesome attitude about yourself first.

That doesn't mean that attitude is everything. It isn't. But I do believe attitude underscores everything.

Here's how I know that: After traveling around the world giving speeches and writing books about my experiences, I've learned that wearing a nametag 24-7 would be utterly useless if I didn't have a great attitude to go with it.

LESSON LEARNED: *It's not about just the nametag; it's the attitude behind it.*

So, why do I have such a great attitude?

Well, because I said so! In other words, self-talk.

Honestly, I felt pretty silly the first few times I did it. Hey, most people do! But I submit to you that the **greatest attitude building habit I have ever undertaken** was to begin my day with daily affirmations.

And I'd like to share mine with you.

What you're about to read is a collection of positive, attitude building affirmations that I've been using every day for years. I read them to myself every morning. Now, you don't have to use these exact phrases. But I hope that by reading them, you are inspired to create your own affirmations that will help you self-talk your way to success:

- *I am an approachable professional.* I will both approach – and be approached by – important people.

- *I choose to maintain an approachable attitude.* I believe that every encounter is one in which I can learn, help others and expand my references, networks and experiences.

- *I feel relaxed.* When I engage with customers, coworkers and friends, they are put at ease and feel comfortable when working with me.

- *I am confident.* When I walk into a room, my smile, body language and appearance project happiness, enthusiasm and joy. I'm sure that wherever I go, I will meet cool, new people; I will learn cool, new stuff; and others will be glad they encountered me.

- *I choose to be easily accessible.* People can get a hold of me without frustration.

- *I am attractive.* Customers and coworkers are magnetized to me because of my superior attitude, ability to make them smile and willingness to assure that they feel comfortable.

- *I have learned to recognize that fear is outweighed by benefit.* Although stepping out of my comfort zone might be tough at first, it's always worth it in the end. And even if I look like an idiot, I know that it's no big deal, and that I'm better because of it.

- *I win small victories first.* In order to develop greater communication confidence, I achieve success in smaller situations first. Then, when I'm faced with something bigger and harder, it is this confidence I draw upon to face these new challenges with enthusiasm and readiness.

- *I will have great day today.* I will do something cool, validate my existence and be myself. I am going to project happiness, enthusiasm, joy, laughter, peace, self-discipline and tranquility today; and as a result, I am going to attract prosperity, abundance, wealth, health and positivity into my life.

- Today is my day and nobody can take it away from me.

CHALLENGE: Create your own affirmations. Read them to yourself every morning for one month.

I know you think that affirmations are totally ridiculous.

I know you think that only chumps do this kind of stuff.

But I also know that my daily affirmations **absolutely changed my life**.

And you wouldn't be reading this book without them.

Get up an hour earlier.

"I'll sleep when I'm dead."

Yogi Berra

The following sentence has made me more money than any other piece of advice I ever received:

Get up an hour earlier.

I'm not going to waste your time explaining it. Just do it.

And if that's not enough, read this:

"In Africa every morning a gazelle awakens knowing that it must outrun the fastest lion if it wants to stay alive.

Every morning a lion wakes up knowing that it must run faster than the slowest gazelle or it will starve to death.

The point is, it makes no difference whether you are a lion or a gazelle: when the sun comes up, you better be running."

— *Unknown*

One hour. That's all I ask.

And if you're wondering what to do with that hour, read on!

Keep daily appointments with yourself.

"It is only when we silent the blaring sounds of our daily existence that we can finally hear the whispers of truth that life reveals to us, as it stands knocking on the doorsteps of our hearts."

K.T. Jong

There are 55 strategies in this book. Right now you are about to read what I believe is the best one. My fave. Numero uno.

Ready?

It's called a Daily Appointment with Yourself. I've been practicing this technique every single day for five years, and I submit to you that **it's the most valuable habit I've ever developed.**

Ever.

It all started in Portland. I moved there after college because 1) I didn't know anybody, 2) I didn't have a job and 3) I'd never been there before.

All good reasons to go, right?

Anyway, I got a job slingin' couches at a discount furniture store. (More on how much I hated this job later). Now, because it was retail, I knew the days would be long, stressful and trying on my patience. So I decided to start "prepping" myself mentally.

Across the street from my apartment on NW Irving was a place called Coffee Time. Every morning at about 7 AM, I grabbed a cup, found a comfortable chair and got myself situated. Then, for the next hour, I did a combination of the following things:

- Journaling my thoughts
- Reading positive, inspirational books
- Reviewing my goals and personal mission statement
- Meditating through breathing exercises
- Praying on the day, my concerns, etc.
- Emptying my mind of all things negative
- Practicing positive self-talk to develop a great attitude (ahem, chapter two)

By the time I finished my appointment, I felt revitalized, energetic, positive, enthusiastic, happy and ready to take on the day. I was mentally prepared to handle anything the world threw at me.

That appointment laid the foundation.

I became addicted. I never missed a day. Even on the weekends. And no matter how busy, tired or stressed I was; there was nothing more critical to achieving daily success than my Daily Appointment. As a result, I developed an amazing attitude that began to attract success, happiness and yes, even money, into my life.

Then one day I overslept.

I think it was a Tuesday. I was running late and didn't have time for my Daily Appointment.

So I skipped it.

BIG mistake.

I missed my bus, forgot to bring my iPod for the commute and ended up rushing to work about 20 minutes late.

I had a terrible day. First one in months. Everything went wrong. I screwed up orders. I snapped at customers. I was annoyed, upset, tired, frustrated and therefore, didn't sell many couches.

Nine hours later I returned home from a day that felt like it would never end. And as I lay on my bed, I knew exactly where I went wrong.

Since then, I've only missed about a dozen daily appointments in five years.

That's how powerful this habit is. It's amazing. And I promise, if you start practicing it every single day:

- You will become less stressed
- You will have fewer bad days
- You will develop a more positive & attractive attitude

So, now that you've got that extra hour (providing you read the last chapter) here are a few guidelines for setting up your own Daily Appointment. Feel free to modify them to best fit your needs:

1. **Solitude.** No conversations. No distractions. You need alone time. If you choose to make your appointment at home, tell everyone else in the house that you're not to be bothered. Treat it like a real appointment with someone very important. Turn off that damn cell phone.

2. **Atmosphere.** Music helps drown out the outside world and enables you to focus on clearing your mind. I suggest calm, soothing sounds.[1] Headphones work best to really pump the tunes into your mind and help you focus.

3. **Supplies.** Depending on your routine, you'll need journals, goal sheets, personal mission statements, positive reading material, headphones, pens, coffee and anything else you need to make this appointment the most comfortable.

4. **Time.** Before work. Before breakfast. Before working out. Before anything. Trust me, the earlier the better. You need to set the stage for your entire day.

5. **Duration.** There is no time requirement, although you can't have much of a Daily Appointment in less than 15 minutes. In fact, a 1999 issue of *Transactional Analysis Journal* revealed that successful people spend at least 15 minutes every day thinking about how they can improve their lives. And if you think you don't have that much time in a day, you're wrong. You don't have the time NOT to do this. Trust me, it's worth every second.

6. **Components.** Although this part is really up to you, some key components include: reading something positive (that means NO newspapers), journaling your thoughts, reviewing goals (HUGE!), doing breathing exercises, practicing daily affirmations and of course, giving

[1] I recommend listening to anything by Thievery Corporation.

thanks. Other activities include praying, meditating, visualizing the success of your day, logging your dreams, etc. Feel free to personalize this appointment according to your needs.

Try it for a month. You WILL notice immediate changes.

Because there's no appointment more important than the one you have with yourself. Every day.

Approachability should be standard operating procedure for all professionals, regardless of age, industry, annual income or job title.

The power of
approachability

*"The most powerful weapon on earth
is the human soul on fire."*

Ferdinand Foch

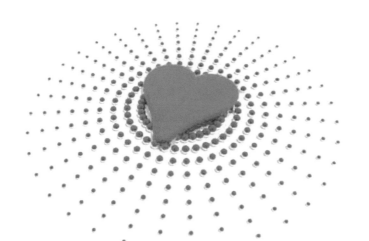

Salt Lake City. September 9, 2006.

I was recovering from a multi-speech day, resting in my hotel room, watching *Anchorman*. I checked the voicemail on my cell. It was from a strange guy named Mike. His message explained that he'd read my first book and would love to chat sometime.

Cool, I thought. And since I'd already seen *Anchorman* seventy-three times, I decided to return his call. A few minutes later, I dialed his number from my cell phone ID. He picked up and said hello.

"Hey Mike, it's Scott, The Nametag Guy!"

"Really?" he asked, followed by a brief silence. "Oh. Hi. Wow, I...uh...really didn't expect you to actually call me back."

Hmmm, I thought.

And so I said to him (in slight confusion), "Mike, why *wouldn't* I call you back?"

"I...I don't know, I guess. I just didn't expect it."

We talked for a few minutes. Pretty cool guy, too. Turns out one of my newest clients was Mike's former boss at the University of Delaware. Small world, huh?

After I hung up, I sat there and wondered: *Wait, why <u>wouldn't</u> Mike expect me to call him back? Isn't that what you do when you get a voicemail?*

We'll come back to that story in a minute. Check out what happened the next day…

I got an email from a potential client who was interested in booking me for an upcoming conference. Excited about the opportunity to work together, I emailed her back two minutes later with my fee schedule, program description and availability.

Sure enough, later on that afternoon, she wrote back to confirm the engagement.

And I kid you not, the exact words in the body of her email: "Wow, I can't believe you actually emailed me right back! Are you sure you're a professional speaker?"

Yes. She actually said that. And again, I was thinking, *Why wouldn't she expect to get an email right back from me? Isn't that what you do when a potential customer inquires about hiring you?*

But wait. It gets better.

Last week I was working in Toledo at an entrepreneur conference. The night before my speech, I went out to dinner with my client and a few of her colleagues from the organization.

"Scott, meet Laura," my client said, "She told me the two of you have already spoken, right?"

"Oh yeah, right!" I said. "I remember our conversation from last week. Nice to meet you in person Laura."

"You too Scott. And by the way, I was really impressed that you actually picked up your cell phone when I called last week. I wasn't expecting that!"

"Really? But why *wouldn't* I pick up the phone?"

"Oh I don't know, I…just…didn't think you would."

OK. Just stop right there. I need to figure this thing out.

I pondered for a minute, scratching my head like I'd been doing something *wrong* this whole time.

And then it hit me. *Holy crap!*

All of these people expect to be ignored because that's the attitude you develop if you actually work in the corporate world.

The world of unreplied emails.
The world of unreturned phone calls.
The world of unapproachable professionals.

Me? I never worked in the corporate world. So how am I supposed to know, right?

Never had a cubicle.
Never had an office.
Never had to fill out TPS reports.

See, I started my company right out of college. No experience. Fresh meat. Untainted by the cruel hands of the white-shirted, red-tied robots featured in Dilbert cartoons.

I guess I just don't know any better.

And I say that in a good way.

See, I do my best to return calls and emails right away because, well, that just seems like the right way to do business.

Like the right way to treat people.
Like the way I would treat my friends.
Like the way I would want to be treated.

Now, maybe I'm naïve. And I'm not perfect. Sure, I forget to call people back sometimes. I have days when I don't feel like talking to anybody. I lose phone numbers, emails and messages just like everybody else. And sure, I'm still under 30. I don't know much.

But I do know that the one compliment I seem to get more than anything is, "Gosh, Scott, you're so easy to get a hold of!"

And the sad thing is, **that should NOT have to be a compliment.** That should be standard operating procedure for all professionals, regardless of age, industry, annual income or job title.

So, do it for me. Do it for yourself. Do it for Dilbert.

Harness the power of approachability.

Discipline breeds discipline.

Discipline is everything.

"The best way to block a punch:
no be there."

Mr. Miyagi

"Hey Scott, have you ever missed a day wearing a nametag?"

Actually, no.

Sure, I've come close many times: walking down the street, jumping into the car or getting out the door and then realizing. "Ah damn it! I forgot to put on my nametag!"

But that's why I carry ten spares in my wallet, bag and car at all times.

So, no, I've never missed a day since November 2, 2000. Which either means I'm incredibly disciplined or incredibly obsessive-compulsive.

Probably both.

But here's the thing. After seven years of wearing a nametag 24-7, one of the strongest and most noticeable changes in my life has been my discipline. For example, I start work every morning around 6 AM. I write for two hours before any calls are made and before any meetings are held. I also read three books a week, pound out dozens of articles and videos a month, meditate daily and somehow manage to post on my blog five days a week.

The result: four books in four years.

And while a lot of my colleagues and clients think I'm crazy, I always say:

> "When you work for yourself,
> discipline is the only boss you've got."

It's the same with exercise. Whether I'm here in St. Louis or traveling around the country, I always find time to run, walk or swim. Even if the conditions aren't ideal. Even if it's really, really hot outside. Even if I get lost in the Rio Grande Park in Albuquerque, lose my room key somewhere in the brush and eventually return to my hotel room three hours later.

Hypothetically.

Still, I think back to the late 90s, or as I like to call it, "BNT: Before Name Tag." My work wasn't as dependable. I didn't exercise consistently. I slept in all the time. And I didn't read or write unless I had to.

But as soon as I starting wearing a nametag, things changed. Formerly annoying tasks and habits became the standard. My discipline grew stronger than ever before! And while I'm not solely attributing my discipline to wearing a nametag, it's certainly helped.

Because discipline breeds discipline.

Another example. Most kids who play sports in high school get better grades than non-athletes. Why? Because if a coach requires his players to practice for three hours after school every day, some of that discipline is going to rub off in other areas.

What about you? What's your discipline?

Consider your business. Pick one discipline you've been practicing DAILY for years. Maybe it's making calls, reading, writing, rehearsing or showing up at the office two hours early before anyone else gets there.

Think about your business BEFORE you started doing that one thing and compare it with your business AFTER that one thing.

Was there a change? Did the discipline breed discipline?

If so, awesome! Keep it up.

If not, don't worry. This is your chance.

> ### LET ME ASK YA THIS...
> Pick something TODAY that you will discipline yourself to doing every single day for the next month. Keep a journal. Watch how the discipline rubs off. It'll blow you away! I'm tellin' ya, this stuff works!

But don't take it from me; take it from Plato. He said, "The first and best victory is to conquer self."

That's exactly what discipline is.

Now, if you'll excuse me, I need to go put on my nametag before I take out the trash.

The best swimmers are always in the pool.

"Our remedies oft in ourselves do lie which we ascribe to heaven."

William Shakespeare

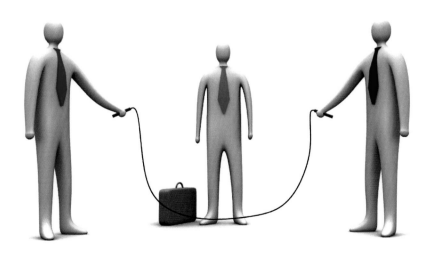

I used to be a Toastmaster.

It was the greatest. Top ten best things I ever did for my career. And although I only had the chance to attend meetings for about six months, I still recommend the organization to everyone.

Even non-speakers.

Especially non-speakers.

Why? It's the perfect organization for networking, enhancing self-confidence and becoming a better *communicator*. Plus, it's really fun.

I recall one particular meeting in late 2004. I was talking to a man named Les. He was a veteran of the organization, but told me that he still came every single week.

When I asked why he said: "Because the best swimmers are always in the pool."

I never forgot that.

The best swimmers
are always in the pool.

Pssst! That's you: the swimmer.

LET ME ASK YA THIS...
How often are you at the pool?

Take necesSCARY action.

"It's normal to get butterflies. The secret is to get them to fly in formation."

Walter Cronkite

"Scott, do you still get nervous before giving speeches?"

Common question.

I usually answer by saying, "Well, I'm a professional speaker. I do this for a living. I'm well researched and trained in the art of public speaking and I've given hundreds of presentations across the world to tens of thousands of audience members for the past several years."

Of course I get nervous.

Every time. Sometimes I even tremble.

That's what I call a necesscary.

Wait. Go back and read the last sentence again. You probably missed it.

Don't worry; that wasn't a typo. You read it right. *Neces-scary.*

I define that as, "Something that you gotta do that scares the hell out of you."

Yes, it's tough.

Yes, it hurts.

But you gotta do it. Frequently. I say every day. Something scary, but something that makes you better.

LET ME ASK YA THIS...
What's your necesSCARY?

Become a student of success.

"Success is a ladder you can't climb with your hands in your pockets."

William James

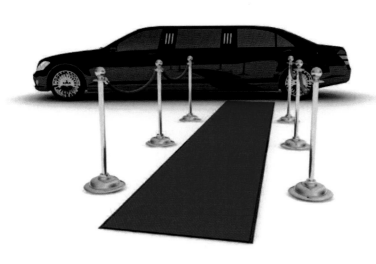

In 2005 when I started asking people the question, "How did you make a name for yourself?" many of them cited their success as a function of **life long learning.**

Of course, this goes well beyond just reading books. It's about becoming a student of success.

In 2002, unsure of how to approach starting my own company, I sought out as many success resources as possible. From reading books to scouring the Internet to interviewing successful people, I was determined to learn the patterns that enabled so many others to make a name for themselves.

NOTE: I'm not talking about duplicating other people's successes. That's impossible. Your goal is to look for patterns, ideas, tips and resources you can apply to your own professional life.

The following is a list of four ways you can become a better student of success.

1)   **Books.** Go onto www.amazon.com and type in the word "success." Last I checked, about 350,000 books came up. Buy a few books each month and DEVOUR them! (They're cheap if you buy 'em used.) Take notes. Highlight key ideas. If you want, you might even try doing it with a group. For example, every Monday, each person could give a five minute book report on success. Or, if you're strapped for cash, just go to your local Borders once a month, type in "success" on their search computer, grab a bunch of books and a notebook and start reading.[2]

2)   **Interviews.** Find smart, successful people who have already made a name for themselves. Ask them questions like:

   • What habits enabled you to become successful?
   • What habits blocked you from becoming successful?
   • What success advice would you give a young professional?
   • What's the best book you've ever read on success?

---

[2]   My editor, Jess, told me that there's also some magical, free place called a "library" where you can "check out books" and conduct research as well. Never heard of it. Go to Borders.

3) **Google.** Spend one hour a week (or more!) on Google. Type in search terms like, "student of success," "success articles" and the like. This is probably your best bet for exposing yourself to a variety of opinions on success. CAUTION: Beware of ideas that contradict each other. Considering triangulating your online research. The Internet isn't always the most reliable source for information.

4) **Personal Exploration.** Keep records of your successes, accomplishments, promotions, big sales, awards and other indicators that you've been making a name for yourself. Update them frequently. Review them often. Consider working with a Success Partner with whom you can share your success tips.

I've been studying success since the day I got out of college. And just like me, you'll discover that when you study success, three things happen:

1. You get excited and motivated about becoming more successful
2. The ideas practiced by other successful people seep into your subconscious
3. And ultimately, you become what you study

School's NEVER out for summer.[3]

---

[3]   My deepest apologies to Alice Cooper.

Play with people
who are better
than you.

Walk with the wise.

*"Whoever walks with the wise becomes wise,
but the companion of fools will suffer harm."*

Proverbs 13:20

Now that you're becoming a student of success, allow me to recommend an effective method for selecting your mentors.

STEP ONE: Initial Contact

Call or email someone you'd like to glean valuable advice from. Introduce yourself. If you have a mutual friend or contact, say that immediately. Explain to the person that you're "young" (in age, job, career, etc.) and would greatly appreciate the opportunity to pick their brain. Suggest a breakfast or lunch meeting.

STEP TWO: Initial Meeting

Look sharp, arrive early and be prepared. Bring something to take notes with and any relevant items you'd like to share with your wise friend. Have a list of questions prepared. Shut up and listen. Take notes furiously. And when the check comes, insist on paying.

STEP THREE: Thank You

The minute you get back to your office, write a thank you note either via email or handwritten. (Handwritten is better.) Promise to keep your wise friend updated on your progress.

STEP FOUR: Progress Report

On a frequent, yet not too annoying basis, call/email the person with an update on your progress. Be sure to tell him or her which pieces of their advice you actually used. If by using that advice you've won an award, made a sale or received any kind of visual representation of success, send them a copy.

REMEMBER: You are (and become) the average intelligence of the people you hang out with the most.

Choose wisely.

Grow
bigger ears.

*"A closed mouth
gathers no foot."*

Mark Twain

I'm sure you don't need me to tell you that the art of listening is **essential** for making a name for yourself. Still, here are my three cents:

1

Listening is not waiting to talk.

2

You have one mouth and two ears. Listen and talk accordingly.

3

A great way to show someone you're listening is to say, "Wait, I don't know what that means."

Thank you.

That is all.[4]

---

[4]   Actually, that isn't all. If you'd like to read a fabulous list of 27 Ways to Grow bigger ears, send an email to scott@hellomynameisscott.com and write "Say what?" in the subject line.

How the world shapes you.

"What people remember about you is who you are."

Sam Horn

You are...

... what you do consistently.

... what you believe.

... what you acquire.

... what you charge.

... what you wear.

... what you eat.

... what you watch on TV.

... what you do for a living.

... what other people say about you.

... what you think about most of the time.

... what you listen to.

... what you blog about.

... what you complain about.

... your experiences.

... your job.

... your mistakes.

... your references.

... your own worst enemy.

... your own best friend.

... your own worst critic.

... who you love.

... who loves you.

... who you hang out with.

... who you choose to be.

... who your parents wanted you to be.

... the books you've read.

... the people you've met.

How does the world shape you?

More books, less TV.

"I've watched TV every day of my life and I turned out TV."

Homer Simpson

Speaking of books…

During my sophomore year of college, my roommate Adam decided to transfer mid-semester. Fortunately he was he was a total asshole and a drug addict who didn't respect my property, so it worked out well.

Anyway, when I returned from class one day, he was gone. His clothes, his posters, everything was gone.

Even his TV.

Oh no, not the TV! I thought.

At first I was scared. *No TV? How will I watch 90210? This is terrible!*

But after a while, I stopped missing it. I found other constructive ways to spend my time, namely, reading books.

After a few TV-less months had gone by, I realized that I was more energetic, more productive, and in general, happier than I'd been all year! Not to mention all the cool stuff I'd learned from reading.

As it turns out, I was onto something. A few weeks later one of my Mass Comm. professors shared two sets of fascinating statistics with the class. The first set came from ACNielsen.

- The average American watches more than 4 hours of TV each day. In a 65-year life, that person will have spent 9 years glued to the tube.
- The number of violent acts seen on TV by age 18 is 200,000.
- The number of 30-second TV commercials seen in a year by an average child is 20,000.
- The number of TV commercials seen by the average person by age 65 is 2 million.
- Rutgers University psychologist and TV-Free America board member Robert Kubey explained that heavy TV viewers exhibited six dependency symptoms - two more than necessary to arrive at a clinical

diagnosis of substance abuse. These included: 1) Using TV as a sedative; 2) Indiscriminate viewing; 3) Feeling loss of control while viewing; 4) Feeling angry with oneself for watching too much; 5) Inability to stop watching; and 6) Feeling miserable when kept from watching.

Unbelievable.

The next set of statistics came from Para Publishing:

- 58% of the US adult population never reads another book after high school.
- 42% of college graduates never read another book.
- 80% of US families did not buy or read a book last year.
- 70% of US adults have not been in a bookstore in the last five years.
- 57% of new books are not read to completion.

Shocking.

Now, you might be skeptical when reading such statistics. (As you should be.)

But whether or not the numbers are accurate, the lesson is obvious:

More books, less TV.

Open a book and you will open your mind.[5]

---

[5]   For a list of 194 Great Books to Make a Name for Yourself, check out the BONUS SECTION at the end of this book.

Even if you're
not a writer,
you're still a writer.

If you write like you talk, readers will listen.

"Be a great date for your reader."

Kurt Vonnegut

Wait a minute. Does that chapter title even make sense? Can readers *listen* to you?

Sure they can. If you write right.

Me, I never took any writing classes. I didn't major in English. And I'm sure my writing isn't as polished as other authors.

So I write like I talk. Like I'm having a conversation with you, right now. And while this isn't the only way to engage readers and help them "listen" to your writing, it's certainly an effective technique.

Kurt Vonnegut once said that to be a great writer, you need to be a "great date for your reader."

Which means you and I are on a date, right now. (By the way, that shirt really brings out your eyes.)

Anyway, back to writing right.

Even if you're not a writer, you're still a writer.

Hey, we all have to do it at some point! And I think the key to capturing your readers' ears (in a non-Van Gogh kind of way) is with your voice.

By "voice" I mean the distinctive quality, feel, sound, cadence and tone of your writing.

Take Dave Barry. He is, in my opinion, the funniest writer in the world. Here's an excerpt from one of his 1996 columns from the *Miami Herald*:

Recently, when I was having a hamburger at an outdoor restaurant, two guys started up their Harley-Davidson motorcycles, parked maybe 25 feet from me. Naturally, being Harley guys, these were rebels — lone wolves, guys who do it Their Way, guys who do not follow the crowd. You could tell because they were wearing the same jeans, jackets, boots, bandannas, sunglasses, belt buckles, tattoos and (presumably) underwear worn by roughly 28 million other lone-wolf Harley guys.

Readers get the feeling that a face-to-face conversation with Dave Barry would be exactly like his writing: hilarious and exaggerated.

So they listen to him. That's probably why he's won a Pulitzer and sold millions of books.

I use Dave as an example because he has a unique voice. Coming from someone who reads three books a week, I'm sorry to say that too few writers understand the value of developing and using their voice.

Because they're afraid. They're afraid of breaking the rules of

grammar and structure. They're afraid of throwing themselves into their art. And they're afraid they'll have to apologize because their writing might offend somebody.

So they hide their true selves behind the same boring, unrevealing, this-is-what-my-English-professor-or-boss-told-me-to-do kind of writing.

Look. I can't tell you how to put more of yourself into your writing. Only you can decide that. Besides, how should I know? After all, this *is* only our first date. Here's a tip or two from the masters:

Leo Tolstoy once said, "Write only with your pen dipped in your own blood."

William Jenkins once said, "Good writing is like walking across a stage naked."

Now ask yourself: "Does my writing reveal who I really am to my readers?" If the answer is no, here are a few ways to start:

1. **Hear it.** Everything you write, read aloud. Decide if it really sounds like you. Imagine you're giving a speech at Harvard's Commencement: would those 5000 students really listen to you?

2. **Notice it.** Pay attention to specific words and phrases used in your daily conversations. Do you also use those in your writing?

3. **Compare it.** Grab a newspaper and read three editorials. What did you like/not like about the voice of the reporters? While reading, did you find yourself completely engaged or thinking about something else?

All writers have a unique voice, whether they use it or not. It isn't something that needs to be created. It's something that's already there. It comes from the heart. All you need to do is *uncover* that voice. And your readers will listen.

Well, this has been a lot of fun. I hope we can go out again sometime...

...how about a kiss goodnight?

The hay is in the barn.

"Life shrinks or expands in proportion to one's courage."

Anaïs Nin

PICTURE THIS: It's exam day. Thirty minutes before test time. And just like every other freaked out college student in the lecture hall, you're squirming in your chair, frantically going over your notes before class begins.

Ten minutes. Five minutes. Then the professor walks in.

And as you shove all your notes under your desk, you say to yourself, "Well, no sense studying anything else. I either know it or I don't."

In other words, **the hay is in the barn.**

I don't remember where I first heard that phrase. Must've been a few years ago. But it means getting to a point where you say, "That's it. I've done everything I can. Nothing I do after this point will improve my performance significantly. It won't get any better. I'm done. The hay is in the barn. Let's do this."

Getting the hay in the barn should always be your goal.

Whether you're preparing for an interview, speech, sales call or your first day at work, you'd better be ready. You'd better have done everything you possibly could to prepare.

When I'm rehearsing, for example, I typically reach this point sometime around 11 PM the night before my talk. Honestly, it's the only way I will be able to sleep that night.

Seriously. Unless the hay's in the barn, I can't sleep a wink because I know I haven't done my best to prepare myself.

That's the way it works. When you get the hay in the barn, a huge weight is lifted. Your stress diminishes. Your confidence soars. You're ready to rock.

HERE'S THE DEAL: You can only prepare so much. So don't kill yourself trying to achieve perfection. Shoot for about 80%. You'll figure out the 20 when you get there.

Small victories first.

*"People are like stained-glass windows.
They sparkle and shine when the sun is out,
but when the darkness sets in their true beauty
is revealed only if there is light from within."*

Elisabeth Kübler-Ross

Small victories build momentum.
Small victories validate self-confidence.
Small victories pave the way for later success.
Small victories enable you to take bolder action.
Small victories stretch your boundaries one mile at a time.

This goes for everything: dating, sports, conversation, business, shyness and speaking in public. For example:

- *If you're terrified of public speaking, try giving a toast at the dinner table of friends and family.*

- *If you're afraid of approaching strangers, go to the mall and strike up conversations with people who won't reject you like clerks, salespeople and cashiers.*

- *If you're reluctant to make sales calls, ring a few stores and ask several product questions to get yourself warmed up.*

- *If you're fearful of writing and publishing articles, start an anonymous blog and post short entries to get used to it.*

- *If you're scared of approaching a cute girl in a bar, try chatting with the cute bartender first.*

- *If you're nervous about giving a speech in front of 300 people, go to a bar and sing karaoke in front of 50 people.*

Small victories first.

A crucial key to making a name for yourself.

To help you put this idea into action, here's a list called **The 5 R's of Small Victories.**

1. **Recognize.** No matter how small, take the time to say to yourself, "That was a victory. I just won. I overcame something that was previously difficult."

2. **Rejoice.** Find a way to celebrate. Get a bell for your office. (I use these and ring it every time I make a sale.) Jump up and down. Say a prayer. Give thanks. Give a high-five to someone.

3. **Record.** Keep a Victory Log. Write down the time, date, type of victory, what you overcame to achieve it and WHY you overcame it.

4. **Review.** At the end of each week, go back through your journal to note your various victories. Give thanks for all of them.

5. **Replicate.** Think about the week ahead: how can you expand those victories into larger successes?

Ultimately, these small victories, when added together, will become the sum total of your continued growth.

Breaking rules trains your mind to create an attitude of creativity, boldness and action.

Rule breakers
rule.

*"First learn the rules so you know
how to break them properly."*

The Dali Lama

RULE: Rock stars have to be larger than life, egomaniac, non-stop partiers who abuse sex, alcohol and drugs.

Right?

Maybe. But try telling that to Chris Martin, front man of Coldplay. Fans, the media - even other musicians – criticize him for being "not enough of a rock star." For being a "sissy" because he doesn't drink, do drugs or take part in typical rock star behavior.

That's funny. Because I distinctly remember Coldplay selling over seven million albums, selling out huge arenas and being dubbed by the music industry as one of the most approachable, down-to-earth and BEST bands of the new millennium. (SPIN, January 2003.)

NEW RULE: Rule breakers rule.

But wait! I'm not telling you to commit any crimes. Don't break *those* kinds of rules! Here's what I mean…

When I first started speaking professionally, my friend and fellow speaker Todd Brockdorf bugged me NON-STOP to join Toastmasters.

(Insert sound of me grumbling.)

I resisted. It seemed too structured. Too many rules. Too many perfectly polished, over-scripted seven minute speeches that didn't make actually me a better speaker.

"Trust me," Todd said, "You need to join Toastmasters. You need to learn the rules so you can break the rules."

(Insert sound of angels signing.)

Amen! Hallelujah! I thought.

So I joined. And, as you learned in Chapter 9, Todd was right. It was awesome.

Therefore, to add a fun sense of irony to this chapter…

The Five Rules of Breaking the Rules

RULE 1: Challenge the validity of the rule. Ask yourself, "Says who?" Google the rule. See if you can find it in writing. Ask 10 people if they've heard of the rule. If not, proceed breaking it.

RULE 2: Question the consequences. Will you or someone else be negatively affected by breaking the rule? Have other people broken it in the past? If so, what happened to them?

RULE 3: Start small. Next time you're out to dinner and your waiter's slacking off, try filling up your own water or iced tea at the busser station. (Trust me, it's exhilarating – I do it all the time!) I GUARANTEE you: nobody will care. In fact, other customers will probably smile as you walk by and admire your boldness. They might even get up themselves.

RULE 4: Keep records. Journal all of the little rules you break over the course of a week. On Sunday, review those rules and ask yourself, "Ok, now did anything bad really happen?" Odds are, the answer will be no.

RULE 5: Think big. By now, you've learned that breaking the rules is ok. (It feels great, doesn't it?) But here's what's happening: **you are training your mind to develop an attitude of creativity, boldness and action.** These small rule-breaking instances are going to accumulate and expand. Eventually, you will start thinking about the bigger picture of your career and life. The status quo. The standards. The boxes the world tries to put you in. And as you continue on this journey to make a name for yourself, you will understand this:

Rule breakers rule.

The most effective way to capture someone's attention (including your own) is to break a pattern.

Break your patterns.

"You can't solve a problem with the same mind that created it."

Albert Einstein

Speaking of breaking things...

Break your patterns. Every day.

This isn't just about creativity. It's about not doing cool stuff. It's about not becoming a slave to routine. It's about spicing up your day, even in the slightest way. It's about enriching your life.

When I slap this nametag on my shirt every day, I never know what to expect. Will a stranger ask me where to find the work shirts in Target? Will a man I've only met via email recognize me while walking down the street, roll down his window and yell "Hey Scott!"?

I use those two examples because both of them happened last Saturday.

Which made me realize something.

Breaking your patterns (daily) is healthy because:

1. It's fun
2. It forces you to think on your feet
3. It stimulates your creativity
4. It gives you new choices
5. It forces you to be more mindful of your surroundings
6. It makes life more interesting
7. It creates cool experiences
8. It shows your vulnerability, and in turn, authenticity

I'm glad (no wait, thankful!) that wearing a nametag 24-7 **forces** me to break my daily patterns.

> **LET ME ASK YA THIS...**
> Which of your patterns did you break this week?

Boredom is the enemy.

"Boredom slays more of existence than war."

Norman Mailer

When was the last time you were bored?

Today?
Yesterday?
Last week?
Last year?

And when you were bored, what did you do?

Eat?
Watch TV?
Doodle on a piece of paper?
Spend an hour on www.boredatwork.com?

I haven't been bored since college. I'm damn proud of that. It's consistently enabled me to accomplish more stuff, meet more cool people and have more fun.

And here's what amazes me: friends and fellow professionals often ask, "Wow! Books, speeches, articles, online videos, blogs, traveling and marketing - where did you find the time to do all that stuff?"

Actually, I never sleep.

No. Just kidding. But last time I checked, all of us had the same amount of time in each day, right?

Maybe it's simply because I wasn't bored.

But don't take it from me. Take it from these guys:

> *Grasp your opportunities, no matter how*
> *poor your health; nothing is worse for*
> *your health than boredom.*
>
> Mignon McLaughlin

*I am never bored anywhere: being bored
is an insult to oneself.*

Jules Renard

*Boredom is like a pitiless zooming in on the
epidermis of time. Every instant is dilated and
magnified like the pores of the face.*

Charlotte Whitton

You get the point: **boredom is the enemy.** Which is kind of funny considering that the world is filled with people who complain, "Gosh, there's never enough time," and people who complain, "Gosh, I'm always so bored!"

Therefore, consider these 16 **MORE's** for eliminating boredom:

1. MORE reading
2. MORE writing
3. MORE blogging
4. MORE exercising
5. MORE masterminding
6. MORE brainstorming
7. MORE networking events
8. MORE reviewing your goals
9. MORE audio learning systems
10. MORE research on the Internet
11. MORE enhancing your creativity
12. MORE lunches with hot prospects
13. MORE reviewing old underlined books
14. MORE calling your clients to check up
15. MORE asking clients why they work with you
16. MORE calling your friends you haven't talked to in months

And if you're still bored,
maybe that means you're a boring person.

Be the only.

Do what nobody else is willing to do.

"I would gladly go down in a flame if a flame's what it takes to remember my name."

John Mayer

Since I started writing this book about two years ago, I've been asking a lot of people to answer one key question: "How did you make a name for yourself?"

A common thread among all the professionals I interviewed was that they "did what nobody else was willing to do."

In other words, whatever it takes.

Check out the following three examples of present-day big shots who did whatever it took to make a name for themselves:

While being raised by his grandmother in the harsh, drug-filled slums of Philadelphia, he dreamed of someday becoming a stand-up comedian. So, he used to sneak into 21+ comedy clubs when he was in high school. He'd watch and study the crowds. He'd watch and study the comics. Eventually he became good enough to start performing at open mics every Thursday night. Fast-forward to 15 years later, his sketch comedy show became the best selling DVD in the history of DVDs.

His name was **Dave Chapelle**.

Then there was the energetic young man from California. His dream was to become the best motivational speaker in the world. So, he started giving speeches three times a day to every Rotary, Kiwanis Club and Chamber of Commerce in town. In two years time, he had ten years experience. Within twenty years, he became not only the best motivational speaker in the world, but a best selling author to boot.

His name was **Anthony Robbins**.

And don't forget about that eager, creative filmmaker who hoped to eventually make it to the big screen. In the 70s, he actually snuck onto the lot of a major movie studio, set up an office and worked there for months! After a while, other producers and directors began to notice him. And in only a few years time, his wish came true.

His name was **Steven Speilberg**.

And the rest, as they say, is history.

Because they did what nobody else is willing to do.

At the time I wrote this book, I'd just finished fourth year in business. And in retrospect, over the years I, too, have done a fair amount of stuff that nobody else was willing to do...

- For the first year or two, I just gave my books away. Literally. Every speech, every networking event, every conversation with a stranger on the plane, free books! Thousands of them! And you know what? It was worth it. Even though a lot of people thought I was crazy not to charge, I knew it was the best way to stimulate word of mouth.

- My first print run was 3000 copies. So, in order to generate more buzz, I hand-glued two nametags on the inside back cover of every book. It was a HUGE pain in the ass and I burnt my fingers a few dozen times, but it certainly got people talking.

- When I first started speaking, to prepare for upcoming speeches I'd stay up all night rehearsing for hours and hours so that my audience didn't think I stayed up all night rehearsing for hours and hours. Which reminds me of what Michael Caine once said, "The art is hiding the art."

- To help pay the bills during those wonderful My Company Isn't Making Any Money Years, I worked nights parking cars at a local hotel. During slow shifts, I

> **LET ME ASK YA THIS...**
> What are you doing that
> nobody else is willing to do?

furiously wrote ideas, articles and stories in my little black journal. My coworkers thought I was crazy! That is, until those scribblings turned into four new books. Including this one.

Consistency is far better than rare moments of greatness.

Discover
a new meal.

*"The secret to getting absolutely
anything you want is simple:
do whatever it takes."*

Mike Hernacki

One of my favorite episodes of *The Simpsons* was the one where Homer attended his twenty-year High School Reunion. During the dinner, he won the award for "Graduate Who Gained The Most Weight."

When the trophy was presented to Homer, the principal asked, "So, Homer, how'd you do it?"

His answer: "By discovering a meal between breakfast and brunch!"

It's always been one of my favorite lines. And silly as it may be, I think Homer makes a good point. Not about food, but about doing whatever it takes.

What about you?

What's your meal between breakfast and brunch?

It's not what you know.

*"I'd rather be known well
than well known."*

Mark Twain

It's not what you know

It's who you know.

It's who you are.

It's who knows you.

It's who you become.

It's who you trust.

It's who trusts you.

It's where you look.

It's how you use it.

It's how you present.

It's how well you know it.

It's how connected you are.

It's what you do.

It's what you want to be.

It's what you can prove.

It's what you don't know.

It's what you know when who you know really needs it!

Speak up or get shut down.

"*We must resist the tendency to believe that the world will come to us, that things will happen to us. We must go to it. We must happen to things.*"

Og Mandino

My flight to Newark was late.
My connecting flight to Geneva took off in 10 minutes.
If I missed my connection, I would miss my speech the next day.

And I was stuck in the **very last seat** on a packed plane.

Not good.

I started to panic. *There's no way in hell I'm going to make it!* I thought.

Then I had an idea. During our descent, I illuminated the call button and explained my situation to the flight attendant. She promised to make an announcement over the PA alerting everyone that a passenger from the back needed to leave immediately to catch an international connection.

We touched down. I clenched my carry on in my lap. My fingers dangled above the seatbelt like a gunfighter from the old West.

The plane taxied to the gate and came to a stop.

But there was no announcement. No warning from the flight attendant. Just the "ding" of the seatbelt sign being turned off. And I watched fifty passengers in front of me stand up and gather their bags.

Not good.

"Hey Scott, what happened to your announcement?" asked the guy next to me.

"Dude, I don't know! I guess she forgot!"

"Well you better do something or else you're never going to make your flight."

He was right. I had to do something.

Then it hit me. I didn't want to do it. I knew it would piss off everyone else on the plane. But I had no choice. No way was I going to miss my speech in Geneva!

At the top of my lungs I announced: "LADIES AND GENTLEMEN, MY FLIGHT FOR GENEVA DEPARTS IN TEN MINUTES AND I WOULD GREATLY APPRECIATE IT IF YOU WOULD PLEASE ALLOW ME TO COME TO THE FRONT OF THE PLANE!"

Everyone stared at me. I gave the cabin one of those "I'm-so-sorry-but-I-have-no-choice" smiles. Finagling my way through the crowd, passengers groaned and shook their heads at me. I started to sweat. I heard one guy say, "Hey buddy, we all have flights to catch."

By the time I got to the front, fifty pairs of eyes burned a hole through my shirt, which was now drenched in my own nervous sweat. The flight attendant waited for me at the door with a big smile on her face.

"Way to speak up, Scott! I've never seen a passenger do that before."

*   *   *   *

I ended up making it to Geneva on time. I gave my speech the next day and rocked the house. Halfway through my presentation, I told the story you just read and concluded with the following piece of advice:

Stand up.

Speak up.

Or get shut down.

Sure, it hurts to find out where you suck.

But I'll take hurting over sucking any day.

Find out where you suck.

"If one person calls you a horse's ass, ignore him. If two people call you a horse's ass, give it some thought. If three people call you a horse's ass, you had better get yourself a saddle."

A Bathroom Stall in the Middle of Ohio

Whenever I submit a new book manuscript to my editor, Jess, I hope she marks up my draft. Like, a lot.

Because I want to know what sucks.

Sure, it hurts. But I'll take hurting over sucking any day.

Also, notice I said to find out "what sucks," not "who sucks."

It's not *the author* who sucks; it's the *writing* that sucks.
It's not *the speaker* who sucks; it's the *delivery* that sucks.

It's not about you. It's about the work.

So, plain and simple: **You need to find out where you suck.**

Take it as free advice to help you improve. Sure, it's harder to ask people to point out the negatives. But this is the only way you're going to get better.

Six Secrets to Finding Out Where You Suck

1. **Pick the right person.** Not everyone possesses the candor to tell you what sucks, i.e., family members. Be careful who you select.

2. **Set ground rules first.** Tell your friend, colleague, etc., that you're looking to improve in certain areas. Ask that they be completely honest and direct with you. Promise there are no hard feelings and that nobody gets defensive.

3. **Take it slow, take it small.** If you saturate yourself with too many Suck Points all at once, eventually it will start to wear on you. So agree to accept feedback in small doses.

4. **Apply.** Don't expect to put everything to use. Apply several of the ideas you feel are valid, throw out the ones that don't work.

5. **Gratitude.** Thank your partner for helping you find out what sucks. Show him how your work has improved by applying his feedback.

6. **Offer to reciprocate.** Be willing to help your friend find out what sucks with her work too. Offer to follow the same guidelines as discussed previously.

Ultimately, I think Jerry Seinfeld said it best, "There are only two types of feedback: 'That's great!' and 'That sucks!'"

If you want to make a name for yourself, you better concentrate on the latter.

Pick up clues when they cross your path, stockpile them in the back of your mind and understand their patterns and meanings.

Life leaves clues.

"The sculpture is already inside the stone."

Michelangelo

When I was seven years old ...

... my teacher made me stand up in front of the class and answer the question, "What do you want to be when you grow up?"

I said I wanted to be an author.

Fifteen years later, my first book was published. Right now, you're reading my fourth.

When I was nineteen years old ...

... I won two awards in my first (and only) public speaking class. One was the award for "Best Speaker," and the other was the award for "Speaker You Could Listen to for Hours."

Three years later, I began speaking professionally. Now, people actually pay me to speak for hours.

Sweet.

This is what happens while you're making a name for yourself:

Life leaves clues.

And you can choose to ignore them.

Or you can choose to pick them up when they cross your path, stockpile them in the back of your mind and understand their patterns and meanings.

Then make your move.

Ask, "Why Me?"

"Those who have not found themselves try to lose themselves."

Earl Nightingale

Any time you are selected, promoted, congratulated, make a sale, secure an interview, get published or accomplish *anything,* you need to ask, "Why Me?"

Don't be shy. Most people are glad to tell you why they picked you. But you need to be proactive. Especially when it comes to:

- Bosses
- Coworkers
- Audience members
- Readers
- Strangers
- Media
- Customers
- Prospects

"Why me?" is NOT an easy question to ask; especially when you've just been promoted, for example. I suggest you pre-empt your inquiry with explanations like:

- "By the way, I'm just curious…"
- "You know, I want to continue this success in the future, so would you be willing to tell me…"
- "Oh, and whenever I work with someone new, it's my policy to ask…"

You need to know the answer to this question.

Not because you're an ego maniac.
Not because you're looking for strokes.
And not because you want to boost your self-esteem.

Because what people remember about you is who you are.

And the reasons people selected you are things you need to duplicate in the future.

My suggestion is to keep a "Why Me?" journal. This will help you discover commonalities among your accomplishments and provide a window for who you are and how you're effectively making a name for yourself.

REMEMBER: Listen to your audience.

Opportunity knocks all the time.

Probably every day.

The problem is that people don't listen.

Become the luckiest person you know.

*"If opportunity doesn't knock,
build a door."*

Milton Berle

Opportunity only knocks once, right?

I used to think so. Because that's what I'd always been told. By the media, by my friends, by my teachers, by everyone.

You only get one shot.
You'll never get a second chance.
Opportunity only knocks once.

Then, after college, I started to get lucky. Like, *all the time*. Lucky with people. Lucky with business. Lucky with life.

- My new neighbor became my best friend.
- I landed huge interviews on CNN and NBC.
- I encountered complete strangers who changed my life.
- I experienced moments of online serendipity that drove millions of people to my website.

Amazing stuff just started happening to me. And I thought, *Man, I'm really lucking out!*

Then I read somewhere that L.U.C.K was an acronym for "Laboring Under Correct Knowledge."

Here's what I think: It's not that opportunity only knocks once. It knocks all the time. Probably every day.

The problem is that people don't listen.

Sure, they might hear it, but they don't take action.

Maybe because they're too busy.
Maybe because they think it's a fluke.
Maybe because they think they're not lucky.
Maybe because they don't think it'll be worth answering.

In short, *pessimism.*

I don't know about you, but I don't *hope* for opportunity. I *expect* it. Every day. Not because I deserve it, but because I've learned how to magnetize and leverage it. In fact, I'd say that I'm the luckiest person I know. And I think I can help you do the same:

6 Steps To Becoming The Luckiest Person You Know

1. **Affirm.** Every morning during your Daily Appointment, affirm to yourself that great things are going to happen to you today. That you're going to experience incredible personal and professional opportunities. That you will be a magnet for cool stuff and people.

2. **Beware.** Always be on the lookout for potential opportunities. Keep your eyes and ears open. Think into the future and ask, "What could this lead to?"

3. **Celebrate.** Whenever one of those "lucky" incidents happens, give thanks. Be excited that you proved yourself right. And say to yourself, I knew this was going to happen!

4. **Documentation.** Write them down. Keep track of your moments in an Opportunity Journal. You might try doing this with a partner with whom you can share your mutual opportunities.

5. **Evaluate.** Look for trends. Figure out what you did right. Figure out what correct knowledge you were laboring under.

6. **Frequency.** If opportunity already knocked once, invite it back. I'm sure it would love to stop by again.

Good luck. May the Schwartz be with you.

Happiness is incidental.

Focus on the umbrella.

*"Most people just see the trees.
I see the forest."*

Sam Walton

I really hate to admit it, but I once watched an episode of *Dr. Phil*.

I know.

Anyway, his advice to the panel of overweight guests was, "Don't dwell on the idea of shedding pounds, but rather, focus on living a *healthier lifestyle*."

He encouraged (er, yelled at) them to modify their eating, drinking, exercising and sleeping habits. And as a result, they would experience increased energy, higher self-esteem, a more positive self-image, and of course, a loss of weight.

They needed be healthy <u>intentionally</u> so they could lose weight <u>incidentally</u>.

I saw that episode two years ago. But it wasn't until this afternoon during an eight mile run in the middle of the mountains – the environment where I always seem to get my best ideas – that I realized how applicable the concept was to business.

I even came up with a cool name for it: **Focus on the Umbrella.**

Take networking, for example. Some people think it's about selling. Or gaining referrals. Or obtaining new clients.

Wrong.

Networking is about the **development and maintenance of mutually valuable relationships.** *The healthier lifestyle. The umbrella.*

Now, sure, while you're networking, it's possible that you'll make a few sales, earn a referral or two or even gain a new client, i.e., losing weight.

But those things happen to you <u>incidentally</u>, not <u>intentionally</u>.

If you focus on the umbrella.

Networking works.

*"It's not who you know,
it's who knows you."*

Jeffrey Gitomer

In my second book, *The Power of Approachability*, I spent a lot of time talking about networking. As you just read a minute ago, networking is "the development and maintenance of mutually valuable relationships."

In my third book, *How to be That Guy*, I also spent a few chapters talking about networking online, or internetworking.

Now, in *Make a Name for Yourself*, you get one chapter about networking. And this is it.

So, here's (almost) everything I know about networking:

1. The Federal Bureau of Labor did a study a few years back indicating that 70% of all new business comes from some form of networking. I think it's higher.

2. No matter where you go — the mall, church, out to dinner, the gym — you better have at least five business cards with you.

3. Be able to give an **UNFORGETTABLE** personal introduction in ten seconds, thirty seconds and sixty seconds.

4. When someone on the phone says, "May I ask who's calling?" get excited. Say something unique that makes that person say, "Um, okay…please hold." Be unpredictable. Be cool. Make the mundane memorable.

5. Get Google alerts on yourself, your company, your area of expertise and your competition. If you don't know what a Google alert is, just Google it.

6. **Networking isn't selling, marketing or cold calling.** It's the development and maintenance of mutually valuable relationships. Don't mix those things up.

7. The most important four letters in the word NETWORKING are W-O-R-K, because that's exactly what it takes.

8. If you give your business card to somebody and they don't reply, "Hey, cool card!" get a new card. (Thank you, Jeffrey Gitomer.)

9. When attending networking events, come early. Check out the nametags. See if you know anybody, or find people you'd like to meet.

10. Sit in the back so you can scan the room for specific people you'd like to connect with.

11. Email articles of interest, links or other cool stuff **OF VALUE** (not spam) to people you've met.

12. Publish a newsletter or ezine. Interview people from your network and feature them as experts. They will take ownership of their inclusion and spread that publication to everyone they know.

13. Spend an hour a week reading and commenting on other people's blogs. If you don't know what a blog is, you're in trouble.

14. When you read an article you like, email the author. Tell him what you liked about it and introduce yourself. He'll usually write back.

15. Have an awesome email signature that gives people a reason to click over to your website. Just be careful not to have TOO much information included.

16. Get involved with social networking sites like LinkdIn, MySpace and Squidoo.

17. Remember that networking doesn't have to be in person. The Internet is a great place to connect with people just like you! It's called Internetworking. (Yep, I made that word up.)

18. Make your own words up. It's really fun.

19. Have business lunches at least once a week.

20. Attend local events once a month.

21. Figure out where your target market hangs out (online and offline). Then hang out there.

22. Create your own regular "business hangout," like a copy or coffee shop where you can regularly be found working, networking, reading or connecting with other professionals.

23. Talk to everybody. Don't sell them; don't probe them, just make friends. Make friends with everybody. Because, as you learned in Chapter 2, people buy people first.

24. Take volunteer positions with organizations that are relevant to your industry. Be a visible leader to whom others can come for help.

25. Every time you meet someone write the letters HICH on their business card: **how I can help**. Then think of five ways to do so.

26. Go to Borders and spend one day a month reading books on networking, interpersonal communication and marketing. I highly recommend *The Power of Approachability* and *How to be That Guy*. (I hear the author is super cool.)

27. Publish articles or a blog or both based around your expertise. Use titles such as "Top Ten Ways," "Essential Elements" and "Success Secrets," that grab the reader's attention. Publish them on www.blogger.com and www.ezinearticles.com

28. Be funny, but don't tell jokes.

29. Discover the CPI, or Common Point of Interest with everyone you meet.

30. Carry blank business cards with you in case someone forgot theirs. They'll thank you for saving their butt!

31. Never leave the house without a pen and paper. Sounds dumb, right? It isn't. It's genius. Nobody keeps napkins with scribblings on them.

32. Every week, introduce two people you know who need to know each other.

33. Wear your nametag above your breastbone and make sure it's visible from 10 feet away. **Nobody cares what side of your chest it's on.**[6] **Just make it big.** And if you don't like wearing nametags, then you probably don't like people knowing who you are, either.

34. Oh, and it's not who you know – it's who knows you. (Thanks again, Gitomer.)

35. And people will like you the minute they figure out how much they ARE like you.

36. Fear not to entertain strangers for by so doing some may have entertained angels unaware. (Hebrews, 13:2)

37. If you don't have www.yourname.com, get it. It's ten bucks.

38. Find local professionals with whom you share common interests, customers, ideas and products. Introduce yourself to them, get together, share ideas and find ways to help each other.

39. Form a mastermind group. No more than four people. Meet regularly to set goals, keep each other accountable and brainstorm.

---

[6] Yes, I know your "supposed" to wear a nametag on the right side of your chest so it's in line with your handshake, but trust me, it's a moot point. Stop worrying about which side of your chest to stick it on. It REALLY doesn't matter. Trust me, I wouldn't have tattooed a nametag on the wrong side of my chest. (That's right. You heard me. I have a tattoo of a nametag on my chest.)

40. Also, set your own networking goals each month for:
    - Events to attend
    - People to meet
    - Emails to write
    - Calls to make
    - Articles/physical mail to send

41. Go onto Google and type in "articles on networking." Read on!

42. Speaking of Google, Google yourself regularly. Find out what people are saying about you. If you don't show up, you're in trouble.

43. If you think you don't need to network, you're right. You don't need to network: you MUST network!

44. **And stop calling it networking.** Ignore the title of this chapter. Networking – as a word – is tired and old and cliché and it makes people think you're throwing around a bunch of cards trying to sell, sell, sell. No. All you're doing is making friends. Not schmoozing, mingling, working the room or any of those stupid catch phrases. You're making friends. That's it. Friends. Make them every day.

45. If you think you suck at networking, don't worry. You're not alone. But also remember that anyone can develop his or her networking skills. That's right, skills. Because it's not something you're born with or just plain "good at." Anyone can do it effectively. You simply need:
    - To develop an attitude of approachability
    - To read books on the subject
    - To practice

46. When strangers ask, "How are you?" don't say fine. F.I.N.E is an acronym for "Feelings I'm Not Expressing." You're not fine. Nobody's fine. Give a real answer that's memorable and magnetic. I suggest, "Business is kicking ass!" or "Everything is beautiful!"

47. Come to every networking event with three great questions ready to go. Be sure they begin with, "What's the one thing…?" "What's your favorite…?" and "What's been your experience with…?"

48. When someone asks where you're from, don't just say "Austin." Use the H.O.T technique: "Oh, I'm from Austin, home of the best college football team in the country." Get creative. Get unique. Watch what happens.

49. Put your person before your profession. Your personality before your position. Your individual before your industry.

50. Think about the last five "luckiest" business contacts you encountered. Figure out what you did right, realize that there IS NO SUCH THING AS LUCK, then repeat as often as possible.

* * * *

REMEMBER: You wouldn't even be reading this book if I hadn't practiced all fifty of the ideas on a daily basis.

Because networking works. Period.

You never know who might be listening, so you better be honest, consistent and authentic.

Word of mouth works.

"Word of mouth is the only honest marketing medium."

George Silverman

Speaking of things that work…

The most fascinating elements about word of mouth are the little stories, encounters and contexts in which it is spread. Me, I monitor my company's word of mouth in a WOM journal. (I suggest you do the same.)

Anyway, the WOM gods have been good to me in the past few years, so here's a list of eleven classic encounters that have boosted sales, increased visibility and enhanced credibility. Enjoy!

JANUARY 18, 2006: Today I did an interview on my local FOX affiliate. How did I secure that spot? Well, the lead anchor for the network was getting his hairs cut by the fiancée of a client of mine. He was telling her a story about a nametag, which prompted her to spend several minutes telling him about my business.

> **THE WORD:** It's not about sneezers, mavens or specific people — everyone spreads WOM. Everyone. All the time. And they do so when you own a word in their minds. Remember: mindshare, not market share.

APRIL 1, 2006: According to one of my clients, the reason she hired me was: her boss left my business card on her keyboard with a sticky note that read, "Get this guy!"

> **THE WORD:** Make your business card SO good that people not only keep it, they show it to their boss.

APRIL 12, 2006: Went to the new Busch Stadium yesterday. Everyone was excited about the Text Message Board. For $2.99 you could send a text message to the number 78364 and minutes later it would appear on the screen for 50,000 people to see. So, on opening day I messaged, "HELLO, my name is Scott!" Unfortunately the screen malfunctioned and I never saw my brand name during the game. However, today my parents went to the game and during the third inning, they saw my message. They called me right away to give me the exciting news. After they hung up, the man sitting next to them said, "Wait, The Nametag Guy is your SON?"

THE WORD: Word of mouth thrives in serendipitous moments.

APRIL 22, 2006: After hearing me speak at a BNI meeting last night, my friend Curt had lunch with one of his out of town colleagues who said, "Hey, have you heard about this guy who wears a nametag all the time?" Curt then spent the rest of the meal reading his speech notes to his colleague!

THE WORD: The best spreaders of WOM are your fans. Again, that's FANS, not customers.[7]

MAY 7, 2006: Today my friend Ed invited me to be a guest at his church. During the sermon his pastor asked everyone in the congregation to "greet their neighbor." When I introduced myself to the guy next to me he said, "Oh yeah, Scott! I know you! You're Ed's friend who wears the nametag."

THE WORD: Word of mouth isn't limited to business hours, or even to businesses! There is a time and place for it: any time and any place.

MAY 25, 2006: Last week I emailed my friend Karen with a link to the story I contributed to in *FastCompany*. As a writer for the *St. Louis Post Dispatch*, she unexpectedly posted my story on her Business Connections Blog. Today my picture and website appeared on the front page of the paper. Wow.

THE WORD: Coverage online often leads to coverage in print.

JUNE 19, 2006: Last night during dinner with my friend and fellow speaker Jeff Magee, I told the story about getting a nametag tattooed on my chest. A few minutes later, the women at the table next to us said, "Excuse me, but, aren't you that guy who wears the nametag all the time? Yeah, I saw you give a speech once! You were great!"

THE WORD: You never know who might be listening, so you better be honest, consistent and authentic.

---

[7] For more information on creating, maintaining and staying in front of your fans, check out my book *How to be That Guy* on www.hellomynameisscott.com. It's fan-tastic!

JUNE 20, 2006: After my speech in Ellensburg, WA today, a woman from the audience told me that she'd just had dinner with a woman who'd seen me speak before. Her friend said, "You've got to get that guy to come to Washington!"

THE WORD: If people say, "Your ears must be ringing!" — well done.

JUNE 23, 2006: Attended a wedding in Chicago this weekend. My childhood friend Andrew introduced me to his girlfriend. She asked why I was wearing a nametag and I told her. She then responded by saying, "Wow! That's so funny. Have you heard about that guy who wears a nametag all the time?" I asked her if I was the guy she'd heard of. She said, "No Scott, it couldn't be you - this guy's CRAZY! He's even got a nametag tattooed on his chest!" I showed it to her. She was speechless. Until she started telling the story to everyone in the room.

THE WORD: If somebody doesn't believe you're the person they've been hearing about, you better be prepared to prove it to them!

AUGUST 12, 2006: Today I got an email from a woman who said, "Scott, I was reading your books on my flight to Houston yesterday. The guy next to me asked about them, so I spent the entire plane ride talking about you! He's going to order several copies for his business!"

THE WORD: Is your idea cool enough that complete strangers would ask someone sitting next to them on a plane what it's all about?

SEPTEMBER 5, 2006: Spoke at a college in Santa Barbara yesterday. My client asked me, "Hey Scott, did I ever tell you how I came across your name? Well, my former partner from Delaware was a big fan of yours. He actually created a program at his university based around your first book that won him an award! He let me borrow it, I went to your website, and three years later, I booked you!"

> **LET ME ASK YA THIS...**
> Keep a WOM journal. Date it. Localize each entry. Figure out the trends, the lessons, the stuff you did right. Repeat often.

THE WORD: It takes time. Sometimes years. But when it catches up with you, it does so in a BIG way.

Everything
is a plus.

"No man's knowledge can go beyond his experiences."

John Locke

My Grandma Mimi is smart.

I was showing her my new condo last year when she made a comment about my decorating. "Scotty, where did you learn how to coordinate colors so well? This place looks great!"

"Yeah, looks like all those days of selling furniture finally paid off," I replied.

"Well, just remember: in life, everything is a plus."

That stuck with me all weekend. *Everything is a plus.*

Kind of reminded me of something Tony Robbins said in *Unlimited Power.*

"Limited references create a limited life. If you want to expand your life, you must expand your references by pursuing ideas and experiences that wouldn't be a part of your life if you didn't consciously seek them out."

I think that's GOT to be one of the most rewarding things about wearing a nametag 24-7: **expanding my references.** Cool things and people and experiences I've encountered that otherwise never would have existed, all of which have had an effect on my life.

From speaking in Switzerland, to having a stalker, to writing a quiz for *Cosmo*, to meeting to 100,000+ strangers, to being inducted into *Ripley's* —
everything is a plus.

THEREFORE:
The more cool/unique experiences you have...
The more cool/unique people you meet...
The more cool/unique things you see, watch, hear, read, taste...
The more cool/unique places you go...
...the more cool/unique you will become.

Everything is a plus. Like my bud Glen Phillips says, "There is nothing that doesn't matter. Every word is a seed that scatters. Everything matters."

Disarm immediate preoccupation.

*"Age is of no importance
unless you are a cheese."*

Glinda, *The Good Witch of the North*

It sucks being a professional speaker under 30.

Actually, not really. I love my job. You couldn't pay me NOT to do it.

But picture this: you're about to walk on stage to address hundreds – sometimes thousands – of seasoned business professionals who are twice your age, have three times your knowledge and four times your experience. Every one of them watches you with skeptical eyes and crossed arms as if to say, "What?! This kid's old enough to be my son! What the hell is HE gonna teach ME?"

Yikes. Talk about stage fright.

In this situation, what you're faced with is called **Immediate Audience Preoccupation.** In other words, "What skepticisms are running through the minds of your audience members before you open your mouth?"

Your mission, should you choose to accept it, is to disarm it.

But it's not just about speeches. This applies to any form of interpersonal communication: conversations, sales presentations, interviews, dates and the like. The following list offers five strategies to disarm immediate audience preoccupation so you can win over skeptical clients and prospects.

Honesty First

My conversation partner's arms are crossed. He's questioning my credibility. He's just waiting for me to prove to him that I'm not the right person for the job.

Tell the truth, tell it all, and tell it now. People will appreciate your honesty, especially when you offer it immediately. What's more, you will validate the credibility of everything you say thereafter.

PERFECT EXAMPLE: Think Peter from *Office Space*.

Provide Social Proof

My price is too high. They're never going to buy. My fee is WAY out of their budget.

Consider sharing testimonials from past clients who *have* paid the full amount and received outstanding return on investment as a result. Instill confidence via social proof that working with you will be worth it.

PERFECT EXAMPLE: Think about the family being interviewed on any home security commercial.

You're Old Enough to be My Kid!

I'm just out of college. Everyone I work with is twice my age. My clients are going to think I'm just some kid.

"A chicken ain't nuthin' but a bird," my Dad always says. Likewise, age is nothing but a number. You're only as old as you act. Remember, you are a professional. Project maturity. And show (don't tell) others about the accomplishments that have enabled you to achieve success. When they see that you know what you're doing, they won't care how old (or young) you are.

PERFECT EXAMPLE: Think Tiger Woods.

Do Your Research

This isn't my industry. This person or audience is completely different than me. I'm clueless about the way they do business.

Google everything. Interview similar people and ask the question, "What's the one thing I could say to someone in your position that would get me in the most trouble?" Then say the opposite. Oh, and don't forget to share your research early. Make people think, "Wow, she did her homework!"

PERFECT EXAMPLE: Think Major League Pitcher before the Big Game.

It's Not the Years, It's the Mileage

I'm new to the industry. I've only been working here a few months. I'm the most recent hire in the entire company.

What's your point? My suggestion: take inventory of your experiences and figure out what unique lessons you've learned and why those lessons benefit your clients.

PERFECT EXAMPLE: Think Tom Cruise in *A Few Good Men.*

REMEMBER: Every audience has some form of immediate preoccupation. If you want to communicate effectively – on stage, in a meeting or even on a date – your duty is to make your audience feel comfortable and confident by disarming that preoccupation as soon as possible.

LET ME ASK YA THIS...

Using these five techniques, come up with ten different ways to disarm that preoccupation.

Love
the haters.

*"Don't hate the player,
hate the game."*

Snoop Dog

While making a name for yourself, about 10% of the people you will encounter will:

Not want you to succeed

Get upset when you succeed

Try to bring you down if you do succeed

I say, "Screw the 10% and focus on the 90."

These people are jealous. They are not making a name for themselves. They have no parade of their own so they're raining on yours. They are haters. And they serve no purpose other than to bring you down, or fuel your own self-belief.

Again, the choice is yours: **get pissed or start laughing.**

Me, I laugh. I even keep my favorite pieces of hate mail on my bulletin board! And I look at them every day to remind me of what Steven Pressfield once said:

"When people see you begin to live your authentic lives, it drives them crazy because they're not living their own."

A-M-E-N!

Love the haters.

Grow thicker skin.

"Nothing shocks me but electricity."

James Brazeau

Speaking of haters…

After all these years, I *still* don't understand why people insult me for wearing a nametag. It just doesn't make sense. I'm trying to make people friendlier for God's sake!

But it happens. Not quite on a daily basis, but every once in a while.

For example, I'd just finished a few days of staff training at the Milwaukee Hyatt. The taxi driver was putting my bags in the trunk when I noticed a group of strange guys standing about fifteen feet away from me.

"Hey Scott!" one of them yelled.

I looked up, waved and answered, "What's up guys?"

As I opened the door to the cab, another guy yelled, "Hey Scott — YOU'RE A DOUCHEBAG LOSER!"

Yes. He really said that. A complete stranger. I started laughing. And as I stepped into the taxi he kept heckling me by saying, "Scott! Hey Scott! Answer me Scott!"

I know. Absolutely ignorant. And while that's one of my more extreme examples, over the years I've encountered thousands of people whose words, whether they were jokes or insults, still hurt my feelings.

(Wow. Did I just say, "hurt my feelings"? That's SO fifth grade!)

Maybe. But you don't have to be kid to have your feelings hurt. It happens to all of us. And what I've learned is: **all that counts is how you react to it.**

I actually looked up the term "thick skin" in the encyclopedia. It's defined as *the ability to withstand criticism.*

I like that.

But I also think people shouldn't ignore criticism; nor should they sit there and take it like a punching bag. It all depends on the source, the validity of the comment made and the *context* in which it was made.

For example, I've received a lot of hate mail over the years. (I know. Makes no sense.) Anyway, most of the people who would leave nasty comments on my blog or send me letters telling me what a loser I was for wearing a nametag…would *never leave their name*. Huh. Interesting.

Clearly these people were ignorant cowards. So, I dismissed their comments.

Anyway, I'm not going to give you a list of all the times people made fun of me for wearing a nametag. That would only bring you down. Besides, I don't think my laptop has enough memory to save all of that.

The point is: thick skin is healthy skin. Furthermore,

Criticism keeps you in check when it's right and keeps you in chuckles when it's ridiculous.

Write that down.

People buy
people first.

Lessons learned from a job that sucked.

"It is far better to make yourself an effective instrument than to know precisely where it's to be used. Temper the iron, sharpen the blade and rest assured, the world will find a way to use it."

Earl Nightingale

As I mentioned, one of my first jobs out of college was at a discount furniture warehouse.

I hated it. Every day was a perfect combination of boredom, back pain and complaints from frustrated customers. The store was hot in the summer and cold in the winter. Most of my coworkers with were twice my age and my boss was a grumpy old jerk.

Fortunately, the pay sucked, I had to work weekends and there were no benefits. (Which was nice.)

But I needed money and I needed experience. *Fast.* So, I sucked it up and did the best I could.

I spent a year there. And although I didn't realize it at the time, I actually learned many lessons about business, sales, customer service and most importantly, how to make name for yourself. Enjoy!

Make a Friend in Thirty Seconds

First thing I learned. My boss said it was the key to retail sales. And since he'd been in the business since, like, the 1850's, I figured he was right.

LET ME ASK YA THIS...

How long does it take you to turn a stranger into a friend?

This principle applies to retail, general sales and networking too. After all, people do business with their friends.

Don't be a Typical Salesman

I shadowed several veteran salesmen for the first week. I studied their approaches, opening lines, closing lines and the like. Then I studied their customers' non-verbal behaviors, emotions and responses.

Guess what I learned? *Customers hate salesmen.* So, I made it my goal to be the atypical salesman in every way I could. (More on this later.)

Think like a Chess Player

I've been a customer before. I know what it's like. So, one afternoon on a slow day, I sat down and made a list of every possible feeling, emotion and assumption made by customers walking through the store.

<blockquote>**LET ME ASK YA THIS...**
Are you like everyone else you work with?</blockquote>

For example: "God I hope the salesman doesn't talk to me..." and "I just want to browse, go away!" By predicting their behaviors, I was able to disarm their concerns. Instead of approaching them, I enabled them to approach me with my own attitude and appearance of approachability.

Bring a Soda

I don't know why, but by carrying a bottle of Diet Dr. Pepper wherever I went, customers seemed to feel more comfortable. The soda made me appear friendly, approachable, casual and not goal oriented. As if I was saying, "Yep, I'm just

<blockquote>**LET ME ASK YA THIS...**
What are your customers thinking about as they walk through the door?</blockquote>

hanging out, drinkin' a pop[8]. If you need anything, I'll be around." *Interesting, huh?*

Be Upfront and Honest

I wasn't on commission. I told that to my customers right away. Most of the time it made them feel comfortable, less intimidated and more willing to work with me.

<blockquote>**LET ME ASK YA THIS...**
What object could help you appear more approachable?</blockquote>

This strategy helped me avoid being a typical salesman because most of my coworkers refused to work with customers who only bought small items. They just wanted the fat commission from the bedroom set. I, on the other hand, treated all customers equally. I just didn't care.

Interestingly, the customers who bought small items from me loved working

---

[8] For the record, I normally refer to carbonated beverages as "soda," but I wanted to use "pop" in this chapter to appease my college friends from Ohio.

LET ME ASK YA THIS...

What truths do you tell the customers right away?

together so much, that they often returned six months later with their kids to buy the bedroom set. And who do you think they wanted them to sell it to them? *Damn right.*

Product Knowledge

During my first few weeks, I walked around the store and made flashcards of every piece of furniture we sold. The cards included descriptions, prices and the like. Over time I was able to speed up my learning curve and memorize every item we offered to better help the customers. I'd even quiz myself on the various products when we were slow. Hell, there was nothing else to do.

LET ME ASK YA THIS...

Are you the expert?

Help Customers Participate

As one of the few young salesmen in the store, I was always assigned the task of moving various couches, loveseats and tables. *Damn it.* And although it was tough on my back, I was able to use the moving process as a sales tool.

For example, if I were sliding a couch into a corner, I'd ask customers walking by, "So, does this look good with that maple table?" or "Could you help me slide this chair around the couch please?" They were almost always happy to help. We'd often end up talking about the decorating process, sore muscles and the like. Instant friends! Also, in many instances, instant sales.

LET ME ASK YA THIS...

How do you get your customers involved?

Unique Openers

I hated phrases like, "Can I help you?" or "Are you looking for anything special today?" And I knew customers hated them too. Let me share with you a list of some of my favorite opening lines that enabled me to make a friend (and often a sale) in thirty seconds:

- While sitting on a couch I'd say to customers passing by, "If you guys have any questions, just wake me up!" or "Don't tell my boss I'm here."

- If someone was looking at the Big Lips Couch (yes, we actually sold stuff like that!) I'd say, "See, when you buy this couch, everyone who comes over to your house will get their ass kissed!"

- Lots of kids came into the store. Instead of trying to sell the parents, I sold the kids. I sold them on ME. This included offering them free donuts or taking "50% off" or "HOT DEAL" stickers and putting them on their shirts. They loved it! The kids AND the parents.

- Because we offered donuts on the weekend, I'd always look for customers who were eating them. Then I'd offer such lines as, "Are you all hopped up on sugar yet?" and "If you spill jelly on this couch, you gotta buy it!" They loved it. Good times.

> **LET ME ASK YA THIS...**
> What's your unique opener(s)?

Unique Closers

I'm not talking about closing the sale. I'm talking about the last thing you say to a customer in your opening conversation that reminds them who you are and that you'd be happy to help. Instead of saying, "I'm Scott if you have any questions," or "Here's my card if you need me," I'd say:

- "If you need anything, I'll be over by the donuts"

- "Well, I'm Scott. If you have an questions, I'll be in the back corner sleeping on the $3,000 Italian Leather Sofa." (SIDE NOTE: one out of every five customers then asked me, "Ooh! Can we see that couch?")

- "I'll let you guys go have fun. If you need me, I'm the only salesman under fifty."

> **LET ME ASK YA THIS...**
> What's your unique closer(s)?

Different is the enemy of unique.

37

Stand out, but don't sell out.

"The first thing you do is figure out the highest price you're willing to pay. Then, the moment someone asks you to pay more, get the hell out!"

Dave Chapelle

THIS SPACE FOR RENT

Five down, one to go.

I was so close to getting the job I could taste it!

All I had to do was ace this last interview and I was a shoo-in for my new position at the Ritz-Carlton.

"OK, Scott, this last question is kind of a tough one. Most applicants usually have trouble with it, so just take your time:

Do you have any weaknesses?"

Damn. That IS a tough question.

Should I lie?
Tell him I don't have any weaknesses?
Or give him the answer he wants to hear?

Well, here goes nothing…

"Sure, I'll give you four of them," I said confidently.

Number one: I'm not a great driver. I know I'm applying for a valet position, but sometimes I make stupid decisions behind the wheel. Heck, I can barely even drive stick!

Number two: I have big eyes. What I mean is, I will scope out every girl that walks through the lobby without realizing that I'm staring. That might get me in trouble with the guests.

Number three: I'm not the most punctual employee. Now, I'm not saying that I'll be late every day, but you'll rarely see me come in early.

Number four: I have a big mouth. I often say silly things that might come off as offensive to others.

But the truth is, sir, all four of those weaknesses I just listed – they can be changed. But the one thing about me that will NEVER change is my **honesty**, and THAT is exactly why you should hire me to work at this hotel.

The next thing I heard was the sound of his jaw hitting the carpet. He looked at me like I just told him I was abducted by aliens from planet Zantar.

After a brief silence, he wrote something down on his legal pad, shifted his weight and leaned back in his chair. He grabbed a quick drink of water and crossed his arms.

I thought I was a goner for sure.

He responded with seven words: GET THE HELL OUT OF MY OFFICE.

Nah, I'm just kidding. What he *really* said was: you got the job!

Initially, I couldn't believe that answer actually worked. But in retrospect, I realize what happened.

I stood out without selling out.

Interviews. Performance evaluations. Meetings. All that stuff. These are opportunities for you to stand out and make a name for yourself.

Which means (yet again) you have a choice:

1. Sacrifice who you are and what you believe, shrink from the opportunity to showcase your individuality and give the guy on the other side of the desk the answer he expected to hear. Or,

2. Summon the courage to be yourself, say how you really feel, fly in the face of convention and stand out like the unique person that you are.

Do. Not. Go. Quietly.

Ever.

If you ever find yourself shaking your head and saying, "What the hell am I doing here?!" ... then you're on the right track.

Remove what robs you.

"Chip away at the barriers that block your abilities and expression."

Benjamin Zander

Prior to working at the furniture store and at the Ritz-Carlton, I also used to be a bartender. It wasn't exactly my number one career choice, but after graduating college and moving to a new city, I needed money FAST.

Besides, *how hard could bartending be, right?*

Here's how terrible I was. In addition to such blunders as "dropping chunks of cork into a customer's Merlot" and "accidentally shattering four pint glasses in front of the District Manager," I was SO bad, that I actually had to consult the Mix Manual to find out what was in a Jack & Coke.

Which made me pretty much the worst bartender in the history of bartenders.

Still, every night I slaved away. And whether I was hurrying around trying to serve drunken customers or frustratingly scraping ABC gum off the underside of the bar, there was only one thought running through my mind:

What the hell am I doing here?! I've GOT to get my first book done...

I lasted six weeks. (I guess the manager made his first mistake when he hired a bartender who didn't drink!) And I remember during my exit interview, Clyde said, "Look Scott, it's just not working out. I'm sure you'll go on to bigger and better things."

He was wrong.

Two months later I started my second job out of college as a floor salesman at the aforementioned furniture store.

And as you just read, it sucked BIG time.

Complaining customers. Pain in the ass boss. No money. Killed my lower back.

I lasted a year. And whether I was desperately attempting to sell a $500 loveseat to a family with three crying children or hiding in the men's bathroom pretending to have a diarrhea so I wouldn't have to work, there was only one thought I running through my mind:

What the hell am I doing here?! I just want to go home and check my email...

Then, in the summer of 2003, two things happened:

1. I quit my job at the furniture store
2. I decided to officially launch HELLO, my name is Scott!

Unfortunately, I learned that there is VERY little money in the speaking/writing when you first start out. Especially if you're twenty-three years old, you have no work experience and you're just some guy who walks around wearing a nametag 24-7 to make people friendlier.

So, while pursuing my writing/speaking career full time, I took a nights/weekends position as a valet parker at the aforementioned Ritz-Carlton.

This job wasn't nearly as bad as bartending or slinging couches. The money was good, the networking opportunities were excellent and Ritz-Carlton ended up being an awesome company to work for.

I lasted two years. A new record for me. (Maybe it would've helped if I knew how to drive stick!) Still, I sucked it up; whether I was running full speed for two straight hours during an 80-car wedding in the 105-degree heat, or standing by the lobby door until 2 AM layered in every piece of clothing I owned during the biting cold of a St. Louis January.

The funny thing is, just like every other job I'd held since college, **that same thought kept running through my mind:**

What the hell am I doing here?! I should be on the phones trying to book speeches...

Eventually, I couldn't take it anymore.

I knew that every minute I'd spent mixing drinks, selling couches or parking cars was robbing me of:

- My true talent
- Chances to further my career
- Time needed to grow my business
- Opportunities to make a name for myself

I made a crucial decision. A decision that everyone, at some point in their career, needs to make:

Remove what robs you, embrace what excites you.

And I never looked back. Best professional decision I ever made.

Now, I know you need to be fair to the Almighty Mortgage. To your family. To your obligations.

But at the same time, **you need to be fair to yourself**. You need to be fair to your talents and gifts.

And if you ever find yourself shaking your head and saying, "What the hell am I doing here?!"

…then you're on the right track.

Remove what robs you, embrace what excites you.

Happiness is _____.

"*Happiness is incidental, not intentional.*"

William Jenkins

A long time ago I saw a bumper sticker that read "HAPPINESS IS HORSES."

I liked it. I liked how specific it was.

Later that day it dawned on me.

Happiness can be whatever you want it to be. And nobody can take that away from you.

That's what's so great about it.

So, at the risk of addressing a vague and difficult topic usually handled by people like The Dali Lama, here goes.

For me, happiness is nametags. Has been for a long time. And while I'm not trying to boil down my happiness to only one source, nametags are definitely a biggie.

Like the smile from a bored, tired cashier's face who says, "Hey Scott!"

Like the childlike curiosity that engages complete strangers to interrupt their patterns, break the silence and ask me a question.

Like the relief I sense when someone who otherwise would've forgotten my name still says hello.

Like the jokes I've heard 10,000 times that make me, the joker, and the other people on the airplane grin, i.e., "Scott, do you have a memory problem?"

I could go on.

The point is; it's been over seven years. Not a single one has gone by during which I wasn't happy, at least for a little while. And sure, I've received a heck of a lot of criticism – even hate mail! - for wearing a nametag 24-7. People accuse me of being weird or crazy. That I just want attention. That I'm just trying to stand out and be different.

Whatever. Let the haters say what they want. My nametag isn't for me; it's for other people. To make *them* friendlier. To make *them* happier. I've merely become incidentally happier in the process because the world is a mirror.

WHAT REALLY MATTERS: I've discovered something that makes me happy. And nobody can take that away from me.

The same goes for you. And I suggest you follow this these four steps for success:

1. Figure out how you would complete to following sentence: "To me, happiness is _____."
2. Make sure the answer doesn't hurt anybody, including yourself.
3. Guard it with your life.
4. Commence happiness.

The moment you realize that you don't need anybody's box is the moment you are set free.

Boxes are for suckers.

"I find it ironic that the phrase 'think outside the box' is an extremely 'inside the box' kind of saying."

Scott Ginsberg

The world will try to put you in a box.

This includes people such as:

- Your parents
- Your friends
- Your coworkers
- Your bosses
- Your competitors
- The media
- Organizations of which you are a member

But,

The moment you realize that you don't need anybody's box is the moment you are set free.

In National Speakers Association, there is a form I fill out which indicates the "topic" on which I speak. There are only about two dozen options. None of them I speak on. There is no box for "approachability" or "being that guy" or "making a name for yourself."

So, I always pick the box that says "other."

Because I don't need no stinkin' box.

And neither do you.

Always pick the box that says, "other."

Write everything down.

"Writing is the basis of all wealth."

Jeffrey Gitomer

And I mean EVERYHING.

- Ideas
- Books to read
- Websites to visit
- Thoughts
- Goals
- Dreams
- Goals (Did I say goals?)
- Lists

Keep journals. Cover the walls of your home and office with Post-it Notes, dry erase sheets and bulletin boards. Keep pen and paper by the toilet, in the shower, in the kitchen, in your car and in your pocket at all times. Use lots of colors, namely, the Sharpie 36-pack. (Trust me, colors stimulate creativity and bring your inner child to the surface.)

EXAMPLE ONE: Ask anyone who knows me: I'm always writing. I NEVER leave the house without my little jotter. My friend thinks I'm crazy. In the middle of dinner, a concert or a baseball game, I'll furiously write something down for ten seconds and then slip the jotter back into my pocket.

This stuff works. For years, I've rarely forgotten an idea or a piece of information, simply because I wrote it down. And part of that has to do with the actual brain function that occurs when you write. For example, did you ever get permission from a teacher in high school to compose a "cheat sheet" for an exam? You spent all night cramming every possible piece of information onto a 3 x 5 card. You didn't even study. *I have the cheat sheet,* you'd think.

Then test time came. And throughout the entire exam, you never once looked at your cheat sheet. It just sat in your pocket. You didn't even need it.

Because the act of concentrated writing actually enables you to retain the information.

LESSON LEARNED: Make more cheat sheets.

And don't forget to review them regularly. That will enable you to:

- Become a more polished writer
- Develop your own unique voice
- Recall stuff you never would have remembered otherwise
- Laugh at some of the crazy stuff you can't believe you actually wrote

LESSON LEARNED: The more often you write, the more evident your growth will be.

EXAMPLE TWO: Every New Year's Day, I read all my journal entries from the previous year. It takes about two hours. And every year, it never fails to blow me away. The stories. The dreams. The accomplishments. The failures. The lists. The complaints. The prayers. Everything running through my mind comes crashing back en masse.

I suggest you do the same. Talk about self-exploration!

It's simple, folks. Write everything down. Everything.

How many cover
bands have ever
been inducted into
the Rock and Roll
Hall of Fame?

Make your own music.

"If you don't have the courage to pursue your own goals, you leave yourself open to the many people who will recruit you to pursue theirs."

Jimmy Calano

During college I spent a number of nights playing music in coffee shops. Nothing too elaborate, just me, my guitar and a microphone. Sharing songs I'd written about stuff that was going on in my life.

By which I mean "girls."

Anyway, it was a singer/songwriter's dream: unplugged, intimate and authentic. Like an episode of VH1 *Storytellers*. The perfect venue to share my art with the world.

The only problem was, people didn't want art. They wanted to hear songs they knew:

"Play some Dave Matthews!"
"Freebird!
"American Pie!"

Right. I'm going to stand up here all night and play covers like some typical, unoriginal, crowd-pleasing, sell out copycat so you and your friends can get drunk and sing along to jams you've heard a thousand times before. If you want that, stay home and listen to your stereo!

Unfortunately, some of them actually did. Or they went to another bar. One of the two.

However, despite smaller crowds, I stayed committed to playing my own stuff. Not because I was the next campus rock star. Not because I was the next Dylan. But because it's just **not in my nature to do other people's material**.

That's just not how I roll. Not in art, not in business and not in life.

I make my own music. Period.

Interestingly enough, after a few years of playing shows, audiences started to *listen between the notes*. People finally embraced the originality of the music. Songs touched them in a new way, even if they didn't know all the words. And ultimately, the art was that much more beautiful. It was sustained by its creativity and uniqueness.

The point is (and we're not just talking about music here):

You can always play someone else's material, but it won't sustain you.

It won't challenge you. It won't expand you. And it certainly won't guarantee you success.

After all, how many cover bands have ever been inducted into the Rock and Roll Hall of Fame?

That's right. Zip-o.

Look. I know sometimes it's just *easier* to play other people's stuff: it's quick, it's safe and it's guaranteed to get you some applause.

But you know what? Receiving a nice round of *inner applause* feels a heck of a lot better.

If you truly want to make a name for yourself, be sure you're making your own music.

Be the world's expert on yourself.

That's how
I roll.

"It ain't what they call you,
it's what you answer to."

W.C. Fields

A few sentences ago you read the phrase, "That's how I roll." What I mean is:

- That's who I am
- That's my M.O.
- That's the way I do business
- That's just me
- That's what you get when you work with me

For example: If I get an email from a company who wants me to give a speech to their employees, I'll call the prospect back within five minutes and say, "Hi Barb, it's Scott, The Nametag Guy!"

Because that's how I roll.

If that company wants to learn more about working together, they'll receive a package from me **the next day** with all the information they need, plus a few free books.

Because that's how I roll.

If I give a speech to that company, I'll come two hours early to meet everyone in the audience, then stay late to hang out with them afterwards. (Duh! I wrote the book on approachability!)

Because that's how I roll.

What about you?

How do you roll?

LET ME ASK YA THIS...

What are you doing on a daily basis to VISUALLY remind your clients, co-workers, bosses, friends and strangers how you roll?

Authenticity, not charisma.

"Keep it real."

Every Rapper Who Ever Lived

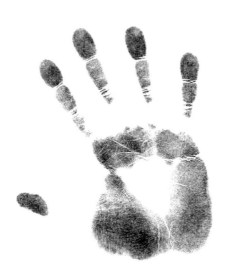

What image would you rather project: *charisma* or *authenticity?*

Charisma comes from the Greek word *kharisma,* which means "gift" or "divine favor." According to Wikipedia, is often used to describe the ability to charm or influence people. It also refers to a quality in certain individuals who easily draw the attention and admiration of others due to a "magnetic" quality of personality and/or appearance.

Big deal. *Hitler was charismatic.* This is 2007. *Charisma will only take you so far.* And in an age of corporate scandal, lack of consumer trust and mass media brainwashing, there is only one attribute that picks up where charisma left off and TRULY magnetizes customers and coworkers to you: **authenticity.**

The word comes from the Latin *authenticus,* or "original, genuine." It's defined as "worthy of trust, reliance, or belief," and it is NOT the same thing as charisma.

An article from the *Harvard Business Review* (Khurana, 2002) explained that while charismatic leaders have often been hired in times of corporate distress, charisma is much more a social product than an individual trait. Furthermore, Khurana explained that "...factors affecting corporate performance are often beyond the powers of even the most charismatic leader."

A related study from Cornell University, which surveyed 6,500 hotel employees worldwide, proved that organizations with employees who rated their managers as "authentic" (not charismatic) were "more profitable than hotels whose managers had gaps between their words and actions."

This is not to say charisma is worthless. I DO think it's a valuable characteristic that many successful businesspeople and leaders possess.

But it cannot stand alone. And here's why...

Lately I've been reading a lot of articles on charisma. And honestly, a lot of them frustrate me.

See, articles written on the topic of charisma usually reference famous political leaders who have innate and exceptional rhetorical/interpersonal skills. As if when it came to charisma, you either had it, or you didn't have it. And if you didn't, well, too bad!

That's why authenticity is more valuable. It doesn't

have such requirements. You don't need to possess the interpersonal charm or brilliance of Bill Clinton to be authentic. You just need to be yourself. And *anybody* can do that to become a more successful communicator and businessperson.

Secondly, many articles written on the topic of charisma are WAY out of date. (5-10 years old.) One piece in particular caught my attention, the writer of which I will not mention because, well, that's just not cool. He said:

"There is a close association between personal charisma and success in life."

What a load of crap.

There are many other determinants of your success besides charisma. I've personally read about (and met) thousands of successful people whom I NEVER would have labeled as "charismatic."

LESSON LEARNED: You don't need charisma to make a name for yourself, but authenticity sure helps.

Figure out exactly who you are, then go out and be that person every day.

On
being on.

Speaking of authentic people…

Quite possibly the best piece of advice I've been given in the past few years came from my friend, mentor and occasional therapist, Richard Avdoian.

"Don't try to be different. In fact, don't try to be anything. Just be. Be yourself. Be the same person no matter where you go. As a result, you WILL be unique. And people will notice. Because there's nothing more approachable than authenticity."

I quoted Richard's words of wisdom during a recent speech. Afterwards, an audience member asked me: "Because you wear a nametag all the time, do you feel like you need to be 'on' all the time?"

On? Like a comedian? An actor? Or a baseball player?

Well, for some people, that would mean every speech, every conversation, every interaction, would have to be like some big performance.

But what does "on" mean, anyway?

For comedians, maybe it means *making people laugh.*
For actors, maybe it means *captivating an audience.*
For athletes, maybe it means *scoring runs or baskets.*

It all depends.

I don't know. Maybe what it really means to "be on" is "to be yourself."

Here's a good example. One of my best friends is Bill Jenkins. I've quoted him a few times in this book, and I referred to him in more detail in *The Power of Approachability* and *How to be That Guy.*

Bill is an author of 25+ books, a preacher, a teacher, a former collegiate baseball superstar and most importantly, a great guy. And I think the reason I admire Bill so much is because I've read his books, taken his classes, heard his sermons, played golf and had countless lunches with him for over ten years.

And he's always the same person. With the exact same voice.

It always sounds like Bill. I hear that same eloquent, selfless baritone in every one of his writings, speeches or even in conversation, and I think, *Man, that's just Bill. He's 100% authentic.*

In other words, he's always on.

HERE'S YOUR ASSIGNMENT: Figure out exactly who you are, and then go out and be that person every day. That's what being "on" is all about.

Zzzzzz...

Zzzzzz...

Zzzzzz...

On being a sleeper.

"It will always be to your advantage to be underestimated."

Donald Trump

January 26, 2006. 11:43 AM.

I was scheduled to deliver the keynote speech at the First International Conference of the Word of Mouth Marketing Association.

I was never more terrified in my life.

The audience was filled with 500 of the smartest, sharpest and most powerful marketing executives in the country. Every one of them was twice my age, had three times my experience and four times my knowledge. I knew it was the most important speech of my career, and I knew that if I blew it, I was TOAST.

Oh, and did I mention that the other three keynote speakers were best-selling authors and CEO's of huge corporations? Yep.

And then there was me. The Nametag Guy. Twenty-five years old. And I thought, *"What the hell am I doing here?!"*

When the president of the organization introduced me he said, "Alright everybody, I want to introduce today's keynote speaker. Now, a lot of you have been coming up to me and asking, 'Where did you *find* this guy?'"

Boy, *there's* a great way to be introduced.

A few seconds later I made my way to the stage. The crowd came to a hush. All eyes were on me. And with my legs still trembling, I paused and smiled for a few seconds before starting the speech.

This is it, I thought. *The opportunity of a lifetime. Just like that song from* 8 Mile.

I absolutely nailed it.

I hit a home run. The performance of my career! And over the next few weeks, it became the most successful, most profitable and most publicized speech I had ever given. That one presentation spring-boarded hundreds of new relationships, dozens of new clients and enough street (web) credibility to last for a lifetime. I even won an award for Best Rookie Performance!

And why?

Because nobody saw me coming. I was the Sleeper.

The Sleeper is a powerful individual. He makes a name for himself under the radar. To find out if you're one of them, explore the following five attributes:

1. **Quiet Confidence.** Sleepers don't brag about big sales they made or large accounts they landed. Then again, they're not bashful about their accomplishments. But take one look at them and you can tell: there's something going on up there.

2. **That Guy.** In my book, *How to be That Guy*, I taught readers how to become somebody who reminded everybody of nobody else. See, that's what Sleepers maintain: uniqueness. Being known for something. Being known AS something. Owning a word in the minds of the people they encounter.

3. **Unexpected Success.** Sleepers aren't the ones you'd look at and expect to make waves. They just do their work and somehow, you hear about it. Then you glance at them and nod, "Wow, nice. Man, I wonder what her secret is…"

4. **Potential to Come Alive.** Sleepers might not be the most recognized people in the office, they might not receive all the glory, but when crunch time comes they always rise to the challenge.

5. **Word of Mouth Worthy.** People talk about sleepers. They get noticed, even if they don't know it. Frequent comments such as, "Keep your eye on that kid!" and "She's someone to watch for this year" are often made in a positive regard for their abilities.

A perfect example of a Sleeper comes from one of my favorite movies, *The Devil's Advocate*. Early in the film, Al Pacino explains his Trial Law Philosophy to Keanu Reeves. During the conversation Pacino has with his young apprentice, he says, "I'm a surprise, Kevin. The jury, the witnesses, and opposing council – they don't see me coming. That's why I win. I'm the hand up Mona Lisa's skirt."

Are you a Sleeper?

On
just being.

*"You are what you pretend to be.
So be careful what you pretend to be."*

Kurt Vonnegut

BE...

... afraid only of standing still.

... regularly silly.

... three moves ahead of everyone.

... unexpected.

... your own definition of success.

... the first one.

... the only one.

... unforgettable.

... remarkable.

... ashes, not dust.

... a sleeper.

... so damn sure of yourself.

... ready for anything.

... the same wherever you go.

... visually accountable.

... the local ball of fire.

... easy to get a hold of.

... consistently consistent.

... the new guy's first friend.

... completely original.

... lightning, not thunder.

... a great conversationalist.

... an even greater listener.

... willing to say, "Wait, I don't know what that means."

... That Guy.

... That Girl.

... your own adjective.

... willing to ask ridiculous questions.

... open to making an idiot out of yourself.

... the brand.

... ubiquitous.

... in front of your fans regularly.

... transparent.

... thick skinned.

BE...

... heard from miles away.

... unique, not different.

... curious, not judgmental.

... approachable; don't work the room.

... a people collector.

... a little crazy.

... not ashamed of your art.

... likable.

... someone your friends can call at 2 AM.

... the first one to show up.

... the last one to leave.

... funny early.

... the best at what you do.

... the only one at what you do.

... impossible to imitate.

... nicer to waiters.

... an engaging storyteller.

... available for Q & A.

... up for anything.

... the only person smiling in traffic.

... Googleable.

... grounded.

... ballsy.

... cool.

... up on the news.

... a person OF character, not just A character.

... a class act.

... a hard act to follow.

... blatantly honest.

... less predictable.

... worth waiting for.

... the greatest.

... the shit.

... the man.

BE...

... quick on the trigger.

... partial to the faces of the wicked.

... better than you used to be.

... tired of complainers.

... the only person singing.

... nicer to the ducks.

... like Bezos.

... a master of something.

... disgusted by smokers.

... sorry less.

... hard to sell.

... easy to please.

... beautiful daily.

... better in concert.

... back and on the attack.

... a stickler for grammar.

... alone daily.

... more patient at the airport.

... slightly famous.

... a sweetheart.

... a better customer.

... part of something cool.

... a heartbreaker once.

... crushed by a heartbreaker twice.

... somebody's mentor.

... nobody's bitch.

... less bored.

... quotable.

... better at small talk.

... radiantly healthy.

... partial to redheads.

... ten again.

... bold or go home.

Somebody's always watching.

"Sometimes I feel like my entire life is one big TV show."

Truman Burbank

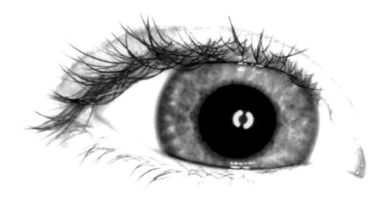

Somebody's always watching.

A friend.
A stranger.
A customer.
A random dude who plays softball with your customer.

Somebody's always watching.

He's waiting for you to wow him.
He's watching to see if you'll screw up.
He's hoping your actions will match your words.
He's anticipating your next move.

Somebody's always watching.

So you better know your stuff. You better be ready in and out of season. And you better not think it won't happen to you.

Because somebody's always watching.

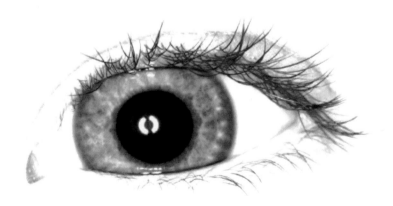

But deep down, he's really a good guy.

"The central criterion of successful personal living is somehow to pass from mere 'multiple selves' into the poise, balance and cohesion of a unified personality."

Harry Emerson Fosdick

Dave might be a jerk…
Dave might be a lazy, unmotivated cheater…
Dave might instigate fights with all the people from HR…
Dave might screw around and get into trouble a lot…

… but deep down, Dave's a really nice guy.

Really?

Well, let me tell you something about Dave (some dude I just made up):

Deep down doesn't matter.
People only give you credit for that
which they SEE you DO consistently.

Think about it. If someone you know is described as, "Deep down, he's a really good guy," odds are that person is "up front, a real asshole."

I once contributed to an article for the *Wall Street Journal*. According to the publication's research, someone you've just met will form a first impression about you in about two seconds.

Two seconds.

Which means that even if you are a really good person "deep down," most of the people you encounter are never going to know it.

So, (as usual) you have a choice:

Maintain unity and congruency
in your personality at all levels
OR
Deep down, just be a "really good guy."

Friendly
always wins.

"Nobody ever got mad at me for being too nice. Except that one guy from New York City who said he'd kill me if ever saw me walking down the street. Good thing I never ran into him."

Scott Ginsberg

In my first book, *HELLO, my name is Scott,* my point was simple: friendly always wins.

I only say that because after all these years of wearing a nametag to make *other* people friendlier, a major improvement I've noticed in my life is:
I've actually become friendlier myself.

The moment you boost your friendliness is the moment you experience the following three payoffs:

1. **People are rarely mean to you.** I've seen the meanest people in the world do complete 180's because of friendliness. This reminds me of Tim Sanders' book *The Likeability Factor.* His research proves that you should never allow yourself to communicate unfriendliness as a first step because, as a social reflex, people will generally reciprocate your friendliness (or lack thereof).

2. **Your cool factor goes up.** A few years back a Canadian University did a study on the link between friendliness and "coolness." They based their findings on a survey of 800 respondents, mostly twenty-something university students. The respondents were asked to rate the coolness of ninety adjectives. They then asked the same respondents to rate the same ninety adjectives according to their social desirability. What they found was a strong correlation between the two. In other words, the qualities that make one socially desirable — being friendly, fair, thoughtful and kind — were also what makes one cool.

3. **Stress is reduced.** Just like you, I've missed flights, lost luggage, received bad service, been cut off in traffic or been knocked into in the middle of a crowded bar. Now, because I'm human, my natural reaction is to get upset. But I rarely do. I always catch a glimpse of that little nametag in the corner of my eye before I yell, "Watch where you're going jerk," and I'm reminded to act friendly. In all these years, I've rarely become SO pissed off to the point of yelling or complaining. Instead, I've learned to react patiently and, most importantly,

in a friendly way. It's never steered me wrong. And I'm sure it's reduced my overall stress level. As a little sub-lesson, that's something I call painting yourself into a good corner.

The point is, even the nicest person in the world can still become friendlier.

The benefits are scientifically based and 100% true.

Friendly always wins.

You don't need to wait for anything or anybody to make a name for yourself.

Wait for nothing.

"Success is waiting for you to make the first move."

John Maxwell

April 17, 2006.

Detroit, Michigan.

I was giving a talk to a group of students at Wayne State University. I'll never forget Tom, the tall guy in the back who asked me, "Scott, what kind of formal training did you have in the areas of giving speeches and writing books?"

Training?

Nothing. Niete. Zilch. Zip. Nada. I just started doing it.

I waited for nothing.

This reminds me of another classic quotation from Og Mandino, one of the world's most beloved (and my favorite) self-help authors. He said in *University of Success*, "Being here is all the permission we need to succeed."

Amen to that!

You don't need to wait for anything or anybody to make a name for yourself.

You don't need to wait for permission.
You don't need to wait for the right time.
You don't need to wait until you get the money.
You don't need to wait for someone else to lead the way.
You don't need to wait for the mainstream to validate your voice.
You don't need to wait until you've had twenty years of experience.

I wrote my first book when I was twenty-two.
I gave my first paid speech when I was twenty-three.

Apparently, that's not the way you're "supposed" to do it.

See, most authors and speakers spend half their lives working for some big company or organization, then decide to write books or give speeches. Not the other way around.

But the age of twenty-two, my thought was, "Dude, I'm not waiting fifteen years. Screw that! I'm ready now. Let's go."

So I did. And looking back, I realize it was the smartest move I ever made.

LET ME ASK YA THIS...
What are you waiting for?

It doesn't matter what music you listen to.

It doesn't matter what you watch on TV.

It doesn't matter which video games you play.

It doesn't matter what college you attend.

It doesn't matter what company you work for.

It doesn't matter what types of people you're surrounded by.

You always have a choice.

You always have a choice.

"The only thing you can control is your choice."

Scott Ginsberg

Throughout this book, you've probably noticed several instances where I explained, "You have a choice."

The reason I repeated that sentence so many times is because I believe:

You become the sum total of your choices.

FACT: You always have a choice
FACT: The only thing in this world you can control is the choice you make.
FACT: The phrase, "you always have a choice," has been one of the strongest, most cherished core values in my life.

That's why I love NCADA. *The National Council on Alcoholism and Drug Abuse* provides the highest quality resources and services that promote a safe and healthy community free of problems associated with alcohol, tobacco and other drugs[9].

NCADA is my favorite non-profit in the world. And here's why.

See, since I was about 12 years old, I've always chosen not to drink, smoke or use other drugs. I'm proud to say that I've never done a drug in my life, never smoked a single cigarette and never abused alcohol.

Now, I'm not saying I have a problem if other people choose to use that stuff. That's up to them. I'm in no position to judge.

It's just not for me.

Anyway, in 2006 I delivered the closing keynote for the Annual NCADA Conference. My final remarks came from a piece I wrote just for that event.

I'm not sure if it's a poem, an essay or a philosophy. But either way, it's called "You Always Have a Choice." Enjoy.

[9] http://www.ncada-stl.org

You Always Have a Choice

When I was a kid...

I used to memorize every dirty lyric to every song on every rap album Eazy-E ever put out.

But I never busted any caps, never spray painted graffiti on public property and never thought it was cool to be a gangster.

When I was a kid...

I used to watch (and record!) every violent, butt-kicking, Van Damme, Arnold Schwarzenegger and Clint Eastwood movie I could find on cable.

But I never raised my fist against someone who insulted me, never caused trouble in school and never got sent to the principal's office for starting a fight.

When I was a kid...

We used to have *The Playboy Channel* at my house. I watched just as many adult films as anyone other teenaged guy would have. (Until my parents disconnected the cable.)

But I never had unprotected sex, never got my girlfriend pregnant and I never thought that sleeping around was worth of bragging about.

When I was a kid...

I use to sit in front of the TV for hours and play every bone-crushing, blood-spattering, automatic-weapon-blasting video game Sega and Nintendo ever put out! (Ahem, *Mortal Kombat*.)

But I never committed a violent act against another person, never bullied any of the younger kids and never thought guns were cool.

When I was a kid...

Most of the people I hung out with smoked cigarettes, used drugs and got drunk every weekend.

But I never touched a cigarette, never used a single drug in my life and never felt the need to get wasted.

When I was a kid...

My college campus was filled with every temptation, every kind of peer pressure and every barrier to responsibility the world could've thrown at me.

But I managed to find my niche, made a name for myself and used what I learned inside (and outside) of the classroom to become a successful entrepreneur.

I'm not telling you these things because I'm perfect.

Trust me, I'm not.

I'm not telling you these things because I've never screwed up.

Trust me, I have.

I'm telling you these things because...

It doesn't matter what music you listen to.
It doesn't matter what you watch on TV.
It doesn't matter which video games you play.
It doesn't matter what college you attend.
It doesn't matter what company you work for.
It doesn't matter what types of people you're surrounded by.

Because when I was a kid, my parents taught me:

You always have a choice.

Three words
of advice.

"My only vice is advice."

Al Pacino

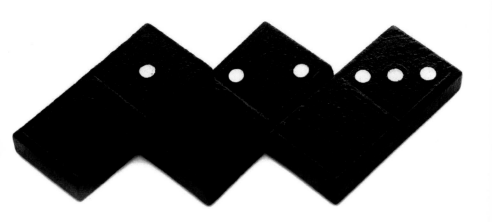

Whew! Almost done. Boy, we sure covered a lot of ground in this book.

I'd like to take this opportunity to do two things. First, to thank you for hanging out with me today. I hope you've enjoying reading *Make a Name for Yourself* as much I enjoyed writing it!

Secondly, to summarize. We've only got a few more chapters to go. And I just love reading books with a section at the end dedicated to recapping the book's key ideas.

In that case, I have **three words of advice** for you:

Abandon popular delusions.	Be a sleeper.
Action develops courage.	Be completely original.
Advertising is dead.	Be one eyed.
And, not or.	**Be regularly silly.**
Anger disturbs action.	Be the ball.
Ask the kids.	Be the only.
Ask dumb questions.	Be visually accountable.
Ask, "What's next?"	Become your beliefs.
Ask, "Why me?"	Break rules more often.
Assault the minute.	Bring it on.
Attain perpetual adolescence.	Build a following.
Attitude isn't everything.	Builders harvest failures.
Attitude underscores everything.	Celebrate the offbeat.
Attract through belief.	Cherish uncertain ground.
Authenticity, not charisma.	Children are teachers.
Avoid the always.	Command a premium.
Balance is bullshit.	Communicate less perfectly.
Ban the bland.	Confidence is king.
Banish the bias.	Consider nothing useless.

Curiosity, not judgment.

Create the fist.

Definitely go there.

Diagnose before prescribing.

Discard old scripts.

Discipline breeds discipline.

Do it anyway.

Don't beat yourself.

Don't get defensive.

Don't jump, pause.

Don't look down.

Don't overeducate audiences.

Do something cool.

Earn inner applause.

Eradicate unhealthy attitudes.

Exercise your mind.

Faith is undefeatable.

Faith trumps fear.

Fans, not customers.

Feed your brain.

Fill the potholes.

Find a way.

Forget the score.

Friendly always wins.

Get a glory.

Get a grip.

Get a Mac.

Get over it.

Get over yourself.

Give value first.

Give yourself away.

Goals, not controls.

Go full time.

Go to Europe.

Grow thicker skin.

Grow bigger ears.

Happiness is incidental.

Holster your fingers.

Honor your gift.

Imagination is everything.

Impossible is nothing.

Inches make champions.

Inspiration comes unannounced.

Interaction, not interruption.

Just do something.

Just have fun.

Know thy power.

Let it go.

Life leaves clues.

Like attracts like.

Love your audience.

Make yourself indispensable.

Market yourself daily.

Medium is message.

Mundane into memorable.

Never be bored.

Never stop laughing.

Nobody notices normal.

Nurture the nuts.

Nurture your nature.

Opportunity knocks daily.

Own a word.

Pay yourself first.

Perception is everything.

Pick a lane.

Plant impossible gardens.

Play solid defense.

Practice, practice, practice.

Prepare for serendipity.

Project impossible patience.

Pursue mindless interruptions.

Reframe your dialogue.

Remember you're mortal.

Respect people's nos.

Respect your hunches.

Responsibilities, not rights.

Right mouse button.

Say affirmations daily.

Say yes more.

Say no more.

Schmoozing is stupid.

Seek nobody's approval.

Self talk works.

Set more goals.

Set yourself afire.

Simple is better.

Small is beautiful.

Small victories first.

Springboards, not straightjackets.

Stick with it.

Stop saying sorry.

Success isn't perfection.

Suck it up.

Surrender your agendas.

Take massive action.

Take more pictures.

Thanks, not sorry.

Think funny first.

Think grandiose thoughts.

Thoughts become blueprints.

Trash the flash.

Travel without plans.

Unique, not different.

Use your life.

Usefulness is worship.

Verbs, not nouns.

Vote yourself off.

Wait for nothing.

Wear your nametag.

We're all salesmen.

What finish line?

Why, not who.

Wisdom, not knowledge.

Write everything down.

You're always marketing.

Food for thought.

"May the most that you want be the least that you get."

Frank Ginsberg

When my grandfather was a boy growing up during the Great Depression, he once found a poem crumbled up in his father's roll top desk. It had such an impact on him, that he kept it and passed it along to his son, my Dad; who then passed it along to me.

Nobody in my family knows who wrote it originally. I even googled it while writing this book and came up with nothing.

I guess that makes this chapter one of the only places you can find it in the world. Check it out:

Food For Thought

The Greatest Sin: fear.

The Best Day: today.

The Biggest Fool: the boy who will not go to school.

The Best Town: where you succeed.

The Most Agreeable Companion: one who would not have you any different that what you are.

The Greatest Bore: one who keeps on talking after he has made his point.

The Greatest Deceiver: one who deceives himself.

The Greatest Invention of the Devil: war.

The Greatest Secret of Production: saving waste.

The Best Work: what you like.

The Best Play: work.

The Greatest Comfort: the knowledge that you have done your work well.

The Greatest Mistake: giving up.

The Most Expensive Indulgence: hate.

The Cheapest, Stupidest and Easiest Thing: finding fault.

The Greatest Trouble Maker: one who talks too much.

The Greatest Stumbling Block: egotism.

The Most Ridiculous Asset: pride.

The Worst Bankrupt: the soul that has lost its enthusiasm.

The Cleverest Man: one who always does what he thinks is right.

The Most Dangerous Person: the liar.

The Most Disagreeable Person: the complainer.

The Best Teacher: one who makes you want to learn.

The Meanest Feeling of Which Any Human Being is Capable: feeling bad at another's success.

The Greatest Need: common sense.

The Greatest Puzzle: life.

The Greatest Mystery: death.

The Greatest Thought: God.

The Greatest Problem Solver: using calm assessment and wise resolve.

The Greatest Thing, Bar None in All the World: love.

If you don't make a name for yourself, someone will make one for you.

(Wait, did I say that already?)

It's not about the nametag.

*"It's not your idea,
it's how you leverage it."*

Scott Ginsberg

In January of 2005 I received the greatest piece of hate mail ever:

> *Dear Scott:*
>
> *Let's face it, buddy: the whole nametag thing is totally stupid. Come on. You've already written a book about it. So what's next? Nothing! You have nowhere to go.*
>
> *You think you're so unique. But there's really nothing unique about wearing a nametag all the time. Anybody could've done that. And there's nothing unique about your book. Anybody could've written that.*
>
> *Good luck (you're gonna need it!)*
>
> *— Greg*

Ouch. That's cold, man.

I wanted to shake it off. I wanted to love the hater, as I mentioned earlier. But I couldn't stop thinking about it. I stayed up all night re-reading that email in my head. Didn't get a wink of sleep. And those four words kept chiming like church bells:

Anybody could've done that.
Anybody could've done that.
Anybody could've done that.

I never told anyone about that letter.

Maybe because I was ashamed.
Maybe because I didn't know the answer.
Maybe because I was afraid Greg was right.

Either way, it didn't resurface until about a year later.

I had just returned to St. Louis after a giving a speech in Orlando. My Dad and I sat down to dinner. We were talking about the growth of my business, writing books, giving speeches and the like. I mentioned the letter.

Then, in this almost eerie, yet proud tone that only a father could project, he said with a nod and a smile, "Scott, it's not about the nametag."

"Huh?"

"It's not about the nametag," he laughed.

"What do you mean?" I asked.

"Well, you've been at this thing going on seven years now. Think about everything that's happened: the company you started, the books, the speeches, the videos, the articles, the change you've brought about to yours and hundreds of thousands of people's lives; everything that's evolved since the day you first stuck that nametag on your shirt. It's pretty remarkable, doncha think!?"

"Yeah, I…I guess it is," I nodded.

"You see Scott, the fact that you wear a nametag every day isn't what makes you unique. Anybody could've done *that*.

But what you've DONE with that nametag, well, NOBODY else could have pulled that off! **And THAT is what makes you unique.**"

So, as we come to a close, I'd like to propose a toast. Here's to you and your journey. And whenever you get to wherever you're going, just remember:

**Don't be friendly,
be approachable.**

**Don't be different,
be unique.**

**Don't be some guy,
be That Guy.**

**As a result, you won't
just be memorable;
you will be unforgettable.**

You will make a name for yourself.

Cool people to thank.

The Production Team

My books and websites wouldn't be *nearly* as beautiful without the help of Jeff Braun, Sue Sylvia, Chris Bradley, Jess "Bagel Girl" Adams, Chad Kouse and CIO Services.

The Fam

I have the greatest family in the history of the world. Period. Thanks for all your support, love and encouragement. By the way, you got any brothers?

The Fans

To all the people who read my books (that's you!), reprint my stuff, watch my videos, hire me to help their organizations and encourage me to continue doing what I'm doing, God bless ya.

The Angel

Garrett, wherever you are, thanks for being That Guy. I still owe you that beer.

The Heroes

For big shots like Seth Godin, Tom Peters, Paul Wesselmann, John Moore, Andy Sernovitz and Jackie Huba, thanks for the inspiration. *Respect.*

The Non-Profits

To my friends and colleagues in SLPA (St. Louis Publishers Association) and NSA (National Speakers Association), thanks for all the ideas, friendships and laughs.

The Board of Directors

Because I can no longer pay homage to merely one mentor, I must thank the following people for their inspiration and wisdom: Shep Hyken, Jeffrey Gitomer, Arthur Scharff, Richard Avdoian, William Jenkins, Andy "Through Others" Masters, "Handsome" Steve Hughes and Carol Weisman.

The Secret Weapon

You know who you are. You melt my butter, baby.

The Musical Inspiration

Special thanks to the following artists whose music inspired me as I wrote this book: Chris Whitley, Mark Sandman, Twilight Singers, Ryan Adams, Jeff Buckley, Glen Phillips, U2, Bruce Hornsby, Bryan Adams, Tool, A Perfect Circle, Ben Harper, Slim Shady, B.R.M.C., Treat Her Right, Death Cab for Cutie, Duncan Sheik, Edwin McCain, Thom Yorke, Jose Gonzales, Kelly Joe Phelps, Mike Doughty, Shawn Colvin, Travis Meeks and Willy Porter.

**Check out the iMix on iTunes called
"Make a Name For Yourself"
to hear the playlist I put together
while writing this book!**

Scott Ginsberg
That Guy with the Nametag

AUTHOR. While only 27 years old, Scott is the author of four books including *HELLO, my name is Scott, The Power of Approachability, How to be That Guy* and *Make a Name for Yourself.*

SPEAKER. As one of the youngest members of National Speakers Association, Scott gives presentations, breakout sessions, keynote speeches and seminars to tens of thousands of people each year. Companies and organizations worldwide have been successfully implementing his unique, informative, entertaining and "use tomorrow" programs since 2003.

DIVERSE CLIENTELE. Since 2003, Scott has worked with large companies like STAPLES, Verizon, Boeing, Prudential Financial, UniGroup, Coldwell Banker, Gundaker Realty, Leo Burnett, Manpower and Hyatt Regency. He's also worked with organizations like International Association of Workforce Professionals, International Cemetary & Funeral Association, American Society of Association Executives, Meeting Professionals International, National Association of Personnel Services, School Nutrition Association, Word of Mouth Marketing Association and The YMCA of America.

NAMETAG GUY. Scott is the only person in the world who wears a nametag 24-7 to make people friendlier. (In case you're wondering, he has a nametag tattooed on his chest for certain occasions.) While transforming his simple idea into a business, his adventures have earned him recognition as "The World's Foremost Expert on Nametags" and secured a spot in *Ripley's Believe it Or Not!*

COLUMNIST. Scott is a regular contributor to the *St. Louis Small Business Monthly, INSTORE Magazine, PR Canada, Small Business TV, Expert Village* and Monster.com. His conversational, content-rich articles have appeared in thousands of online and offline publications worldwide. Also, his work has been reprinted in dozens of textbooks and resource guides.

MEDIA EXPERT. Dubbed as "The Authority on Approachability," Scott is regularly interviewed by various online, print, radio and TV media for his unique expertise. He has been featured in outlets such as *CNN, USA Today, The Wall Street Journal, Inc. Magazine, The Associated Press, FastCompany, The Washington Post, Paul Harvey, The CBS Early Show* and *Headline News.* He even wrote "The Quiz" on approachability for *COSMO!*

NAMETAG NETWORK. Scott's award winning, content-rich websites get as many as 30,000 hits a day from readers and audience members around the world. His ubiquitous web presence and powerful platform set the standard for entrepreneurs and marketers in his field, and have earned him an surprising amount of credibility seeing that he's just some guy who wears a nametag every day.

Scott lives in St. Louis, Missouri, where he often talks to strangers.

Bonus Section

194 Great Books to Help You Make a Name for Yourself

1001 More Ways You Reveal Your Personality, Elayne Kahn

50 Success Classics, Tom Butler-Bowdon

A Better Way to Live, Og Mandino

A Kick in the Seat of the Pants, Roger von Oech

A View from the Top, Zig Ziglar

A Whack on the Side of the Head, Roger von Oech

A World of Strangers, Lyn Lofland

Aha! Jordan Ayan

All Business is Show Business, Scott McKain

All Marketers Are Liars, Seth Godin

Are You Positive? Richard Gaylord Briley

As a Man Thinketh, James Allen

Asshole No More, Xavier Crement

Be Your Own Brand, David McNally & Karl Speak

Better Than Good, Zig Ziglar

Better Together, Robert Putnam

Blink, Malcom Gladwell

Bowling Alone, Robert Putnam

Brain Tattoos, Karen Post

Bravely, Bravely in Business, Richard Connarroe

Building the Happiness Centered Business, Dr. Paddi Lund

Choices that Change Lives, Hal Urban

Communicate with Confidence, Diane Booher,

Consulting for Dummies, Bob Nelson & Peter Economy

Contact, Leonard Zunin

Conversation, Theodore Zeldin

Conversationally Speaking, Alan Garner

Cracking Creativity, Michael Michalko

Dickless Marketing, Yvonne DiVita

Dig Your Well Before You're Thirsty, Harvey McKay

Don't Be Shy, Claude Clement

Emotional Intelligence, Daniel Goleman

Enthusiasm Makes the Difference, Norman Vincent Peale

First Impressions, Ann Demaris & Valerie White

Freakonomics, Steven Levitt & Steven Dubner

Free Prize Inside, Seth Godin

Future Diary, Mark Victor Hansen

Games People Play, Eric Berne

Get Slightly Famous, Steven van Yoder

Goodbye to Shy, Leil Lowndes

Grapevine, Dave Balter

Growing Your Business, Mark LeBlanc

Habits of Wealth, Bill Byrne

Happiness is Smiling, Katherine Gehm

He's Just Not That Into You, Greg Behrendt & Liz Tucillo

Help for Shy People, Gerald Phillips

Here's My Card, Bob Popyk

How to be a People Magnet, Leil Lowndes

How to Click with Everyone Every Time, David Rich

How to Connect in Business in 90 Seconds or Less, Nicholas Boothman

How to Give a Darn Good Speech, Phillip Thiebert

How to Make a Habit of Succeeding, Mack Douglas

How to Make People Like You in 90 Seconds or Less, Nicholas Boothman

How to Start Conversations & Make Friends, Don Gabor

How to Win Friends and Influence People, Dale Carnegie

IdeaSpotting, Sam Harrison

In Search of Excellence, Tom Peters &

Influence, Robert Cialdini

Interaction Ritual, Erving Goffman

It! Jeffrey Magee

It's in the Cards, Ivan Misner

Join Me! Danny Wallace

Just Do This Stuff, Larry Winget

Life After College, Andy Masters

Love is the Killer App, Tim Sanders

Make a Name for Yourself, Robin Fisher Roffer

Masters of Networking, Ivan Misner & Don Morgan

Masters of Success, Ivan Misner

Million Dollar Consulting, Alan Weiss

Million Dollar Habits, Brian Tracy

Money Talks, Alan Weiss

Naked Conversations, Robert Scoble & Shel Israel

Network Your Way to Success, John Timperley

Networlding, Melissa Giovagnoli & Jocelyn Carter-Miller

Never Be Lied to Again, David Lieberman

New Rules, Bill Maher

New Think, Edward de Bono

Nobodies to Somebodies, Peter Han

On Being a Real Person, Harry Emerson Fosdick

People Skills, Robert Bolton

Perfect Phrases for Managers & Supervisors, Meryl Runion

Permission Marketing, Seth Godin

Pop! Sam Horn

Positive Thinking Every Day, Norman Vincent Peale

Power Speak, Dorothy Leeds

Professional Networking for Dummies, Donna Fisher

Psycho Cybernetics, Maxwell Maltz

Purple Cow, Seth Godin

Put Your Best Foot Forward, Jo-Ellan Dimitrius

Radical Careering, Sally Hogshead

Re-imagine, Tom Peters

Relations in Public, Erving Goffman

Remember Every Name Every Time, Benjamin Levy

Rich Dad, Poor Dad, Robert Kiyosaki

Road Trip Nation, Mike Marriner and Nathan Gebhard

Secrets for Success and Happiness, Og Mandino

Secrets of the Millionaire Mind, T. Harv Ecker

See You at the Top, Zig Ziglar

Self-Disclosure, Sidney Jourard

Self-Promotion for the Creative Person, Lee Silber

Sell Easy, Thomas Winninger

Shut Up, Stop Whining and Get a Life, Larry Winget
Six Thinking Hats, Edward de Bono
Small is the New Big, Seth Godin
Social Intelligence, Daniel Goleman
Stay Alive All Your Life, Norman Vincent Peale
Succeed on Your Own Terms, Herb Greenberg & Patrick Sweeney
Success Built to Last, Jerry Porras, Stewart Emery & Mark Thompson
Success, One Day at a Time, John Maxwell
Take this Advice, Sandra Bark
Talking the Winner's Way, Leil Lowndes
The 100 Absolutely Unbreakable Laws of Business Success, Brian Tracy
The 100 Greatest Business Ideas of All Time, Ken Langdon
The 100 Simple Secrets of Happy People, David Niven
The 100 Simple Secrets of Successful People, David Niven
The 22 Immutable Laws of Marketing, Al Ries & Jack Trout
The 7 Powers of Questions, Dorothy Leeds
The Anatomy of Buzz, Emanuel Rosen
The Art of Possibility, Benjamin Zander
The Art of Winning Conversation, Morey Stettner
The Attention Economy, Thomas Davenport, John Beck
The Bible, Various Authors
The Brand Called You, Peter Montoya
The Brand You 50, Tom Peters
The Choice is Yours, John Maxwell
The Choice, Og Mandino
The Complete Idiot's Guide to Clear Communication, Kris Cole
The Culture of Fear, Eric Schlosser
The Death and Life of American Cities, Jane Jacobs
The Difference Maker, John Maxwell
The E-Myth Revisited, Michael Gerber
The Fine Art of Small Talk, Debra Fine
The First Five Minutes, Mary Mitchell
The Game, Neil Strauss
The Good Book, William Jenkins
The Greatest Miracle in the World, Og Mandino
The Greatest Salesman in the World, Og Mandino

The Greatest Salesman in the World: Part 2, Og Mandino

The Greatest Secret in the World, Og Mandino

The Greatest Success in the World, Og Mandino

The Hidden Dimension, Edward Hall

The Integrity Advantage, Adrian Gostick & Dana Telford

The Law of Success, Napoleon Hill

The Likeability Factor, Tim Sanders

The Little Black Book of Connections, Jeffrey Gitomer

The Little Red Book of Sales Answers, Jeffrey Gitomer

The Little Red Book of Selling, Jeffrey Gitomer

The Medium is the Massage, Marshall McLuhan

The Obvious Expert, Elsom & Mark Eldridge

The Personal Branding Phenomenon, Peter Montoya

The Positive Principle Today, Norman Vincent Peale

The Power of Charm, Brian Tracy & Ron Arden

The Power of Positive Thinking, Norman Vincent Peale

The Presentation of Self in Everyday Life, Erving Goffman

The Pursuit of WOW, Tom Peters

The Return of the Ragpicker, Og Mandino

The Richest Man Who Ever Lived, Steven Scott

The Rules of Business, FastCompany Magazine

The Search to Belong, Joe Meyers

The Search, John Battelle

The Seven Habits of Highly Effective People, Steven Covey

The Success Principles, Jack Canfield

The Tipping Point, Malcom Gladwell

The Transparency Edge, Barbara & Elizabeth Pagano

The Transparent Self, Sidney Jourard

The Ultimate Secret to Getting Absolutely Everything You Want, Mike Hernacki

The Virtual Handshake, David Teten & Scott Allen

Think and Grow Rich, Napoleon Hill

Thinkertoys, Michael Michalko

This is Earl Nightingale, Earl Nightingale

Total Self-Confidence, Robert Anthony

Tribal Knowledge, John Moore

Triumph Over Shyness, Murray Stein & John Walker

Trump Your Way to the Top, Donald Trump

Try Giving Yourself Away, David Dunn

Turning to One Another, Margaret Wheatley

Unhooked Generation, Jillian Straus

University of Success, Og Mandino

Unleashing the Ideavirus, Seth Godin

Upgrade! Mark Sanborn

What Do I Say Next? Susan Roane

What Should I Do with My Life? Po Bronson

When They Were 22, Brad Dunn

Why We Don't Talk to Each Other Anymore, John Locke

Wisdom for a Young CEO, Douglas Barry

Wisdom to Grow On, Charles Acquisto

Words that Win, Don Gabor

Wrestling with Success, Jeffrey Gitomer and Nikita Kolof

Yay, You! Sandra Boynton

You Can If You Think You Can, Norman Vincent Peale

You've Only Got Three Seconds, Camile Lavington

Your Attention Please, Paul Brown & Alison Davis

Your Best Life Now, Joel Osteen

Your Road Map to Success, John Maxwell

HELLO, my name is Scott Resources

Books
HELLO, my name is Scott
The Power of Approachability
How to be That Guy
Make a Name for Yourself

Ebooks
8 Golden Ideas to Magnetize Success
25 Self-Motivating Messages to Stimulate Sales
37 Ways To Be Approachable, Be That Guy and Make a Name for Yourself
55 Great Questions to Ask Someone You Just Met
66 Priceless Pieces of Business Advice I Couldn't Live Without
117 Phrases That Payses to Exude Approachability
203 Things I've Learned about Writing, Marketing & Selling Books
234 Things I've Learned about Creating, Delivering & Marketing Speeches

Visit www.hellomynameisscott.com and other sites in
The Nametag Network to learn about corporate discounts!

For information about speaking engagements, books,
online learning materials (or just to say hey), contact Scott at:
HELLO, my name is Scott!
7563 Oxford Drive #2 South
St. Louis, MO 63105
W: (314) 256-1800
C: (314) 374-3397
scott@hellomynameisscott.com

That's the package.